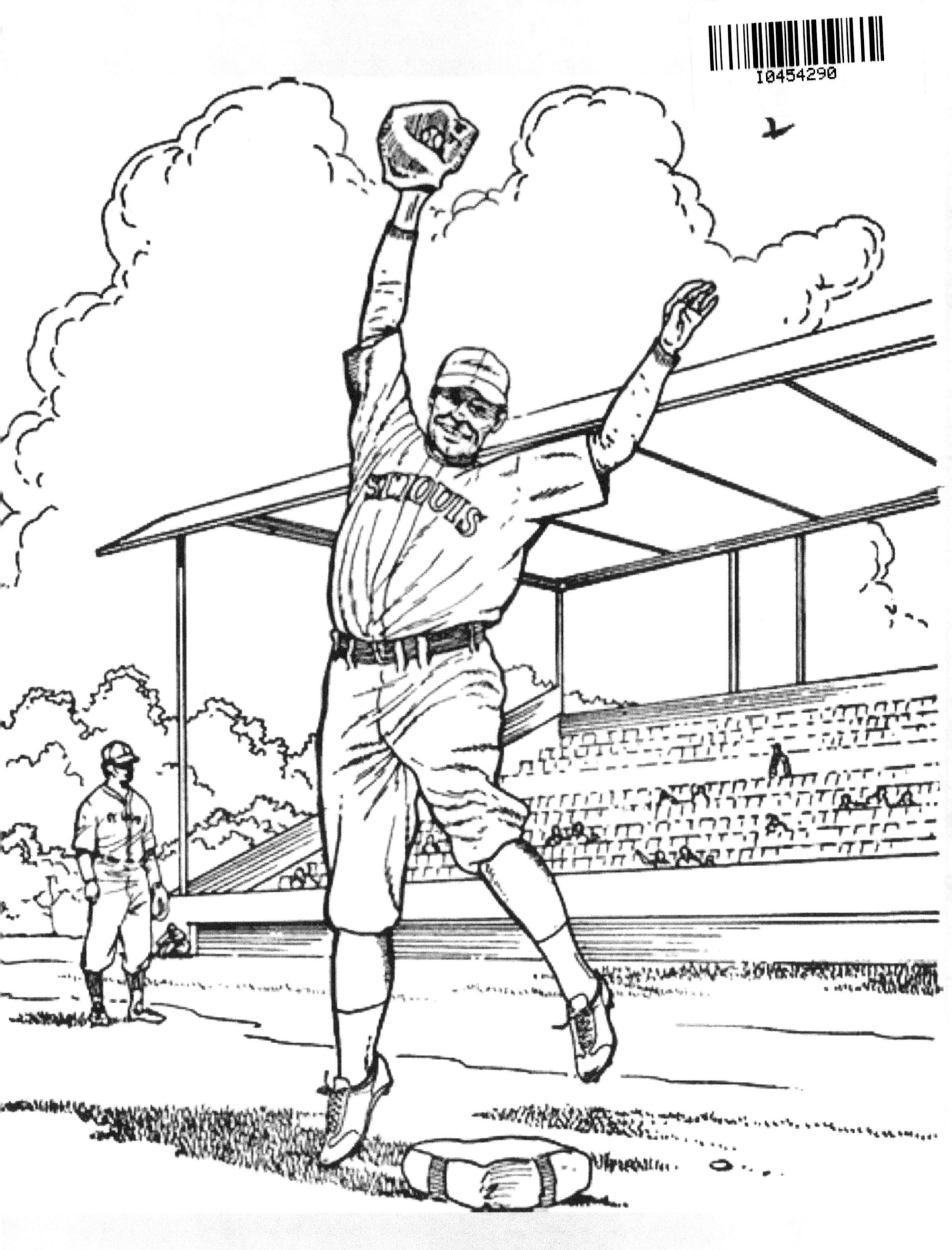

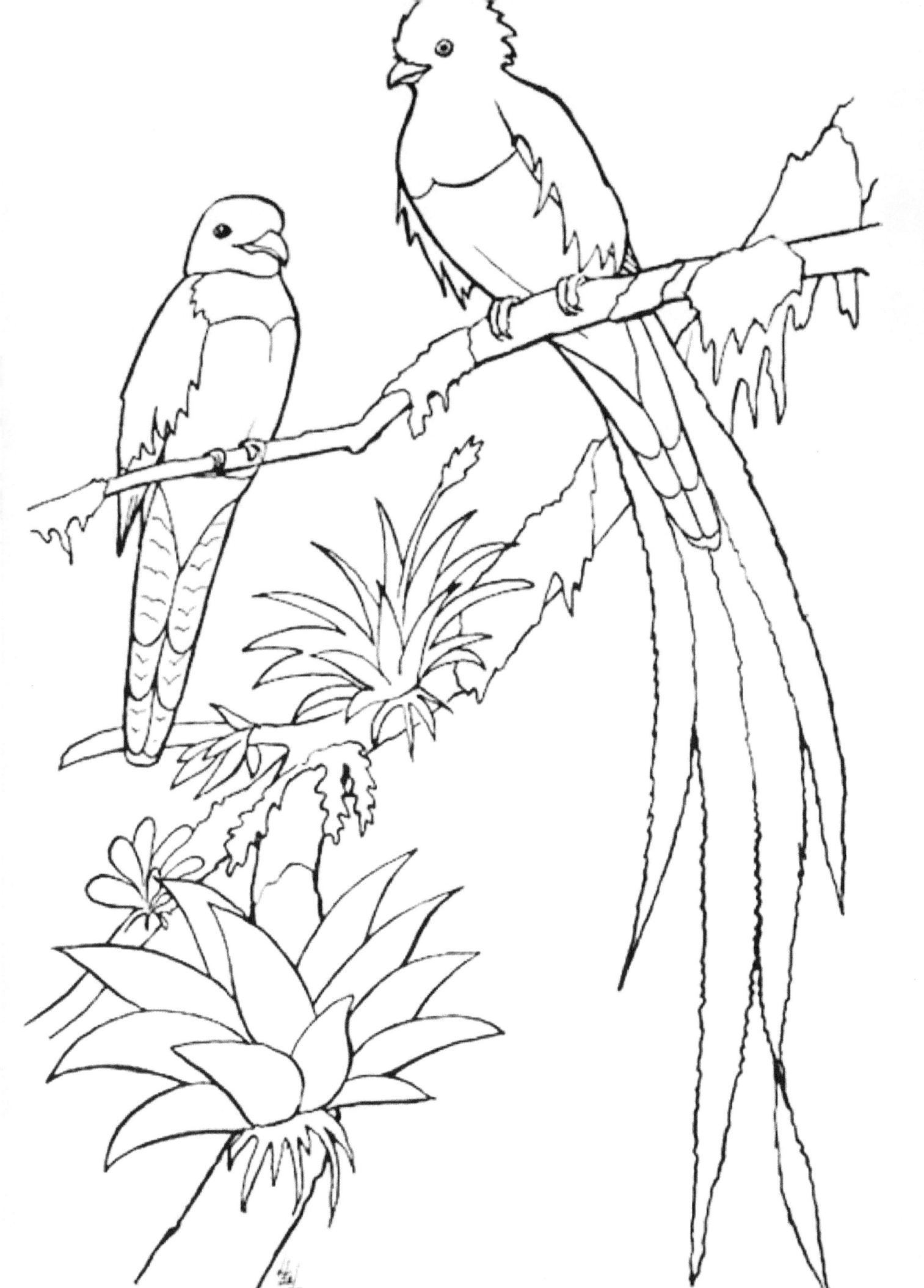

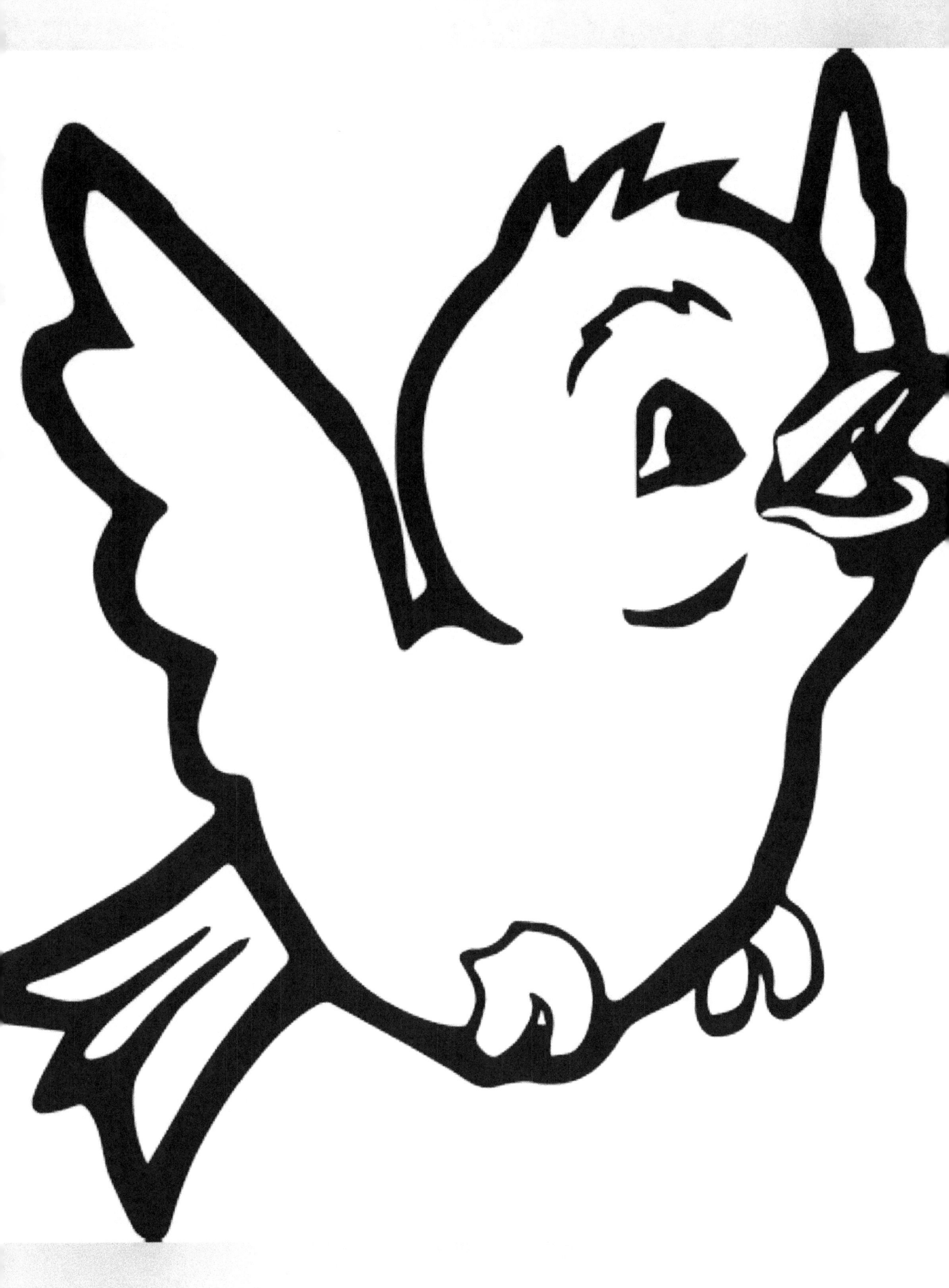

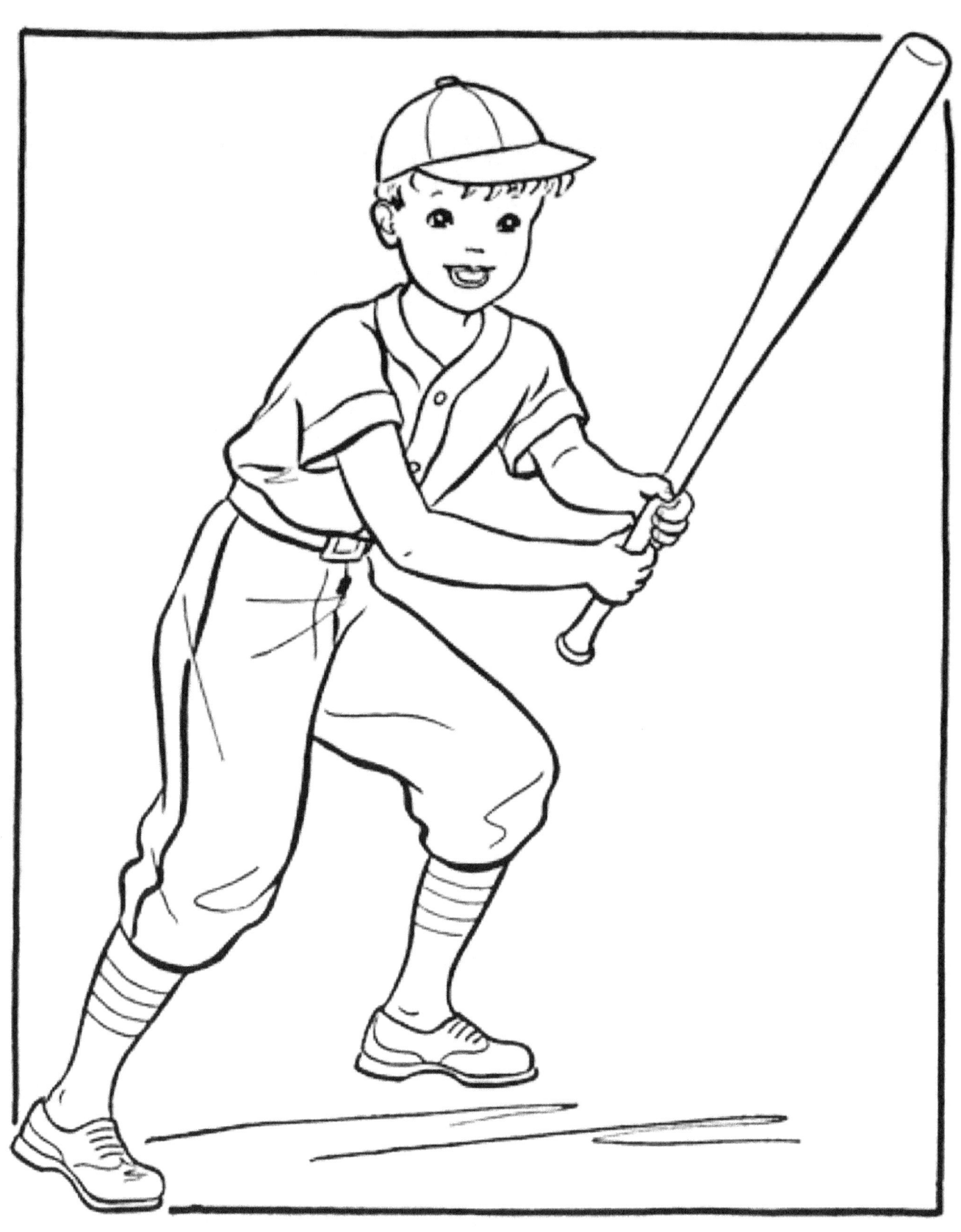

Hit a Home Run, Bob!

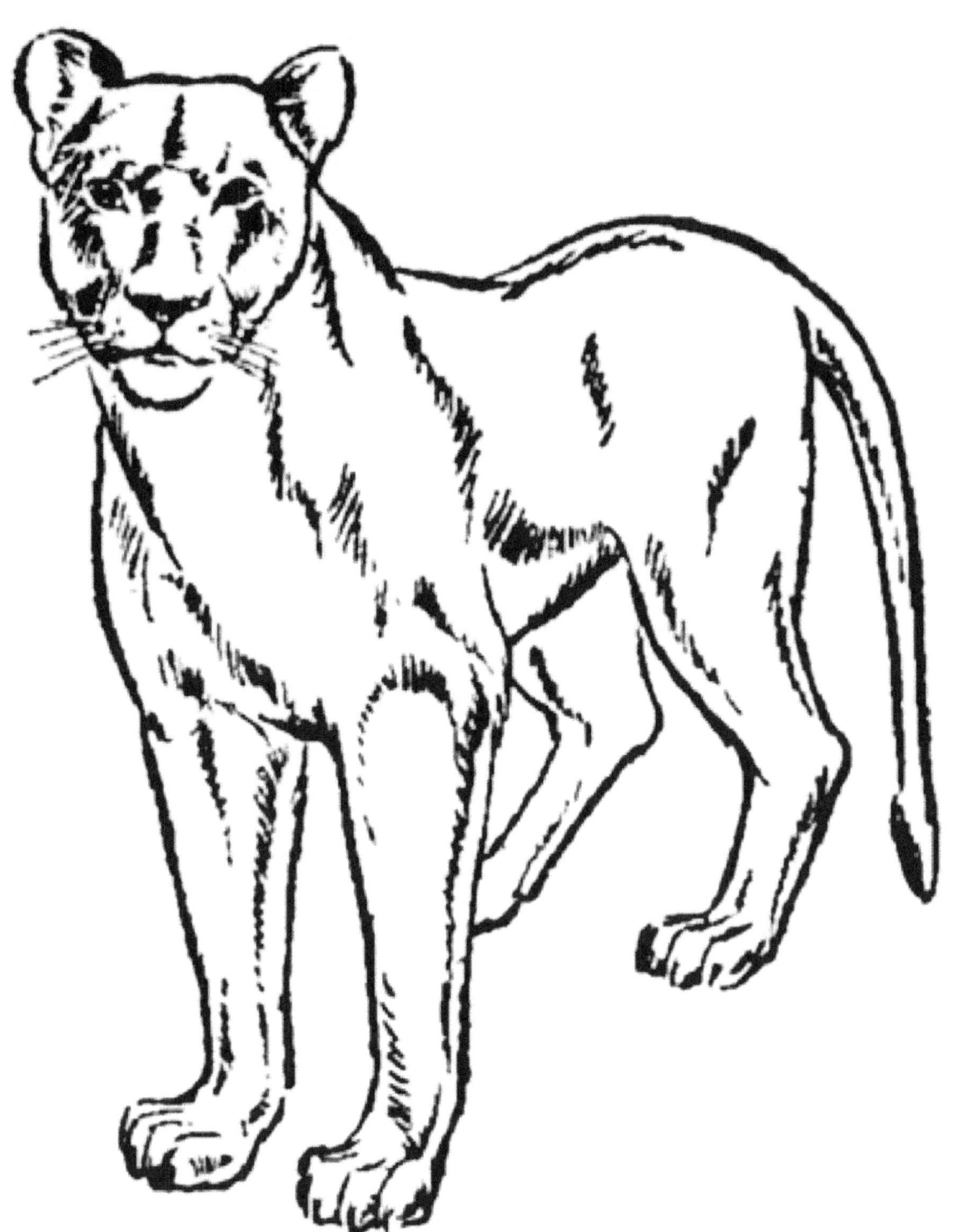

LION
Golden-tan

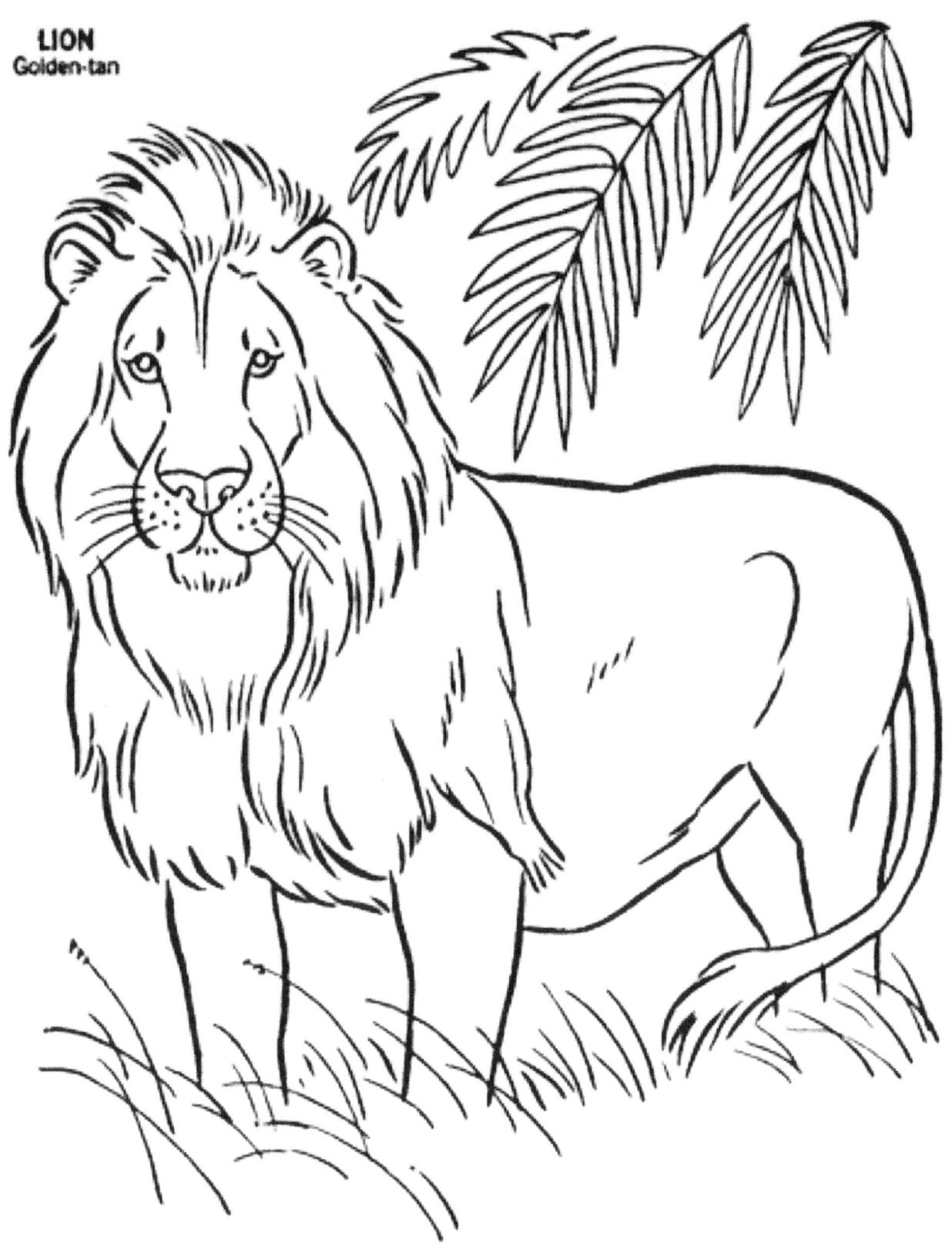

The king of animals prefers deserts and plains to the jungles.

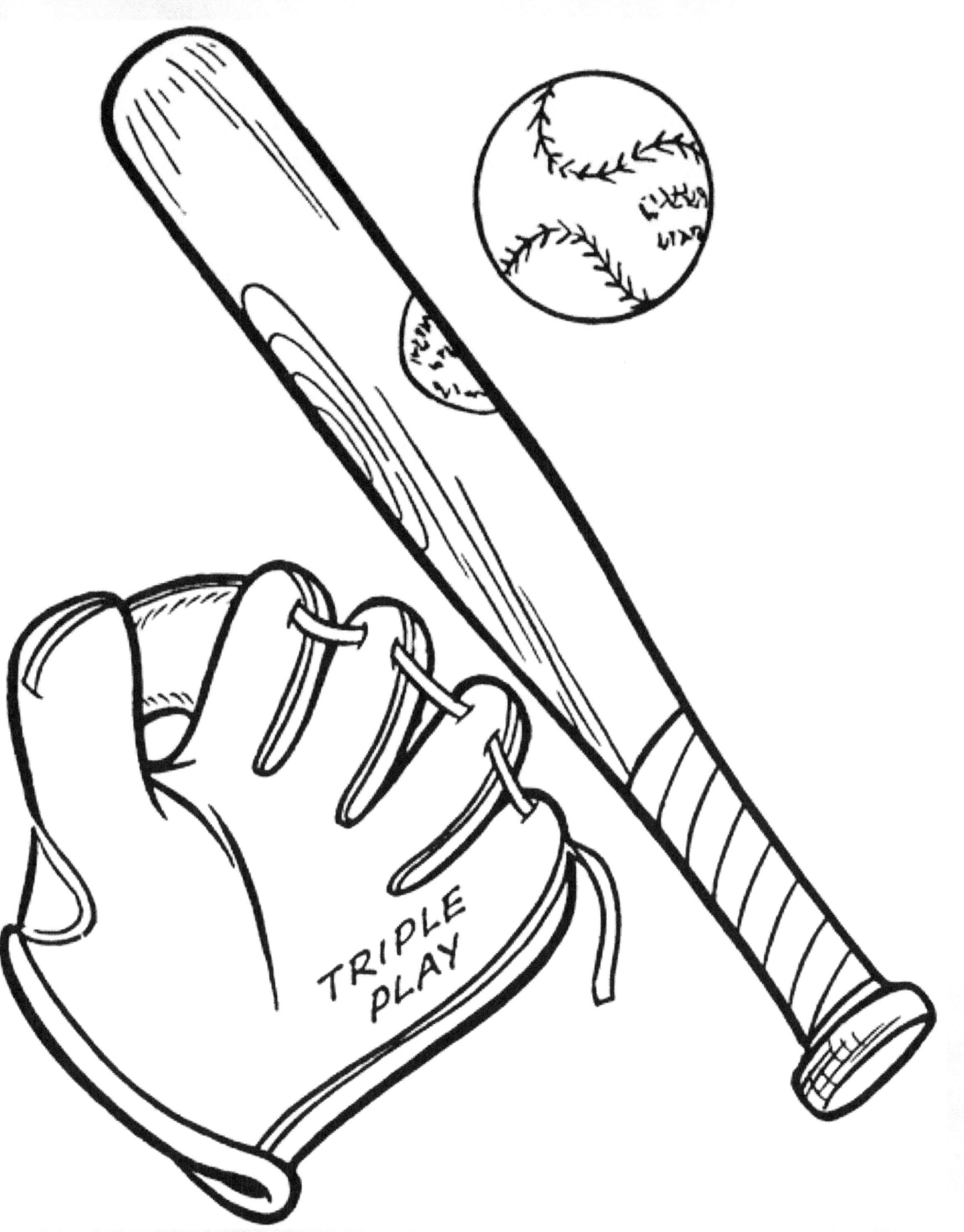

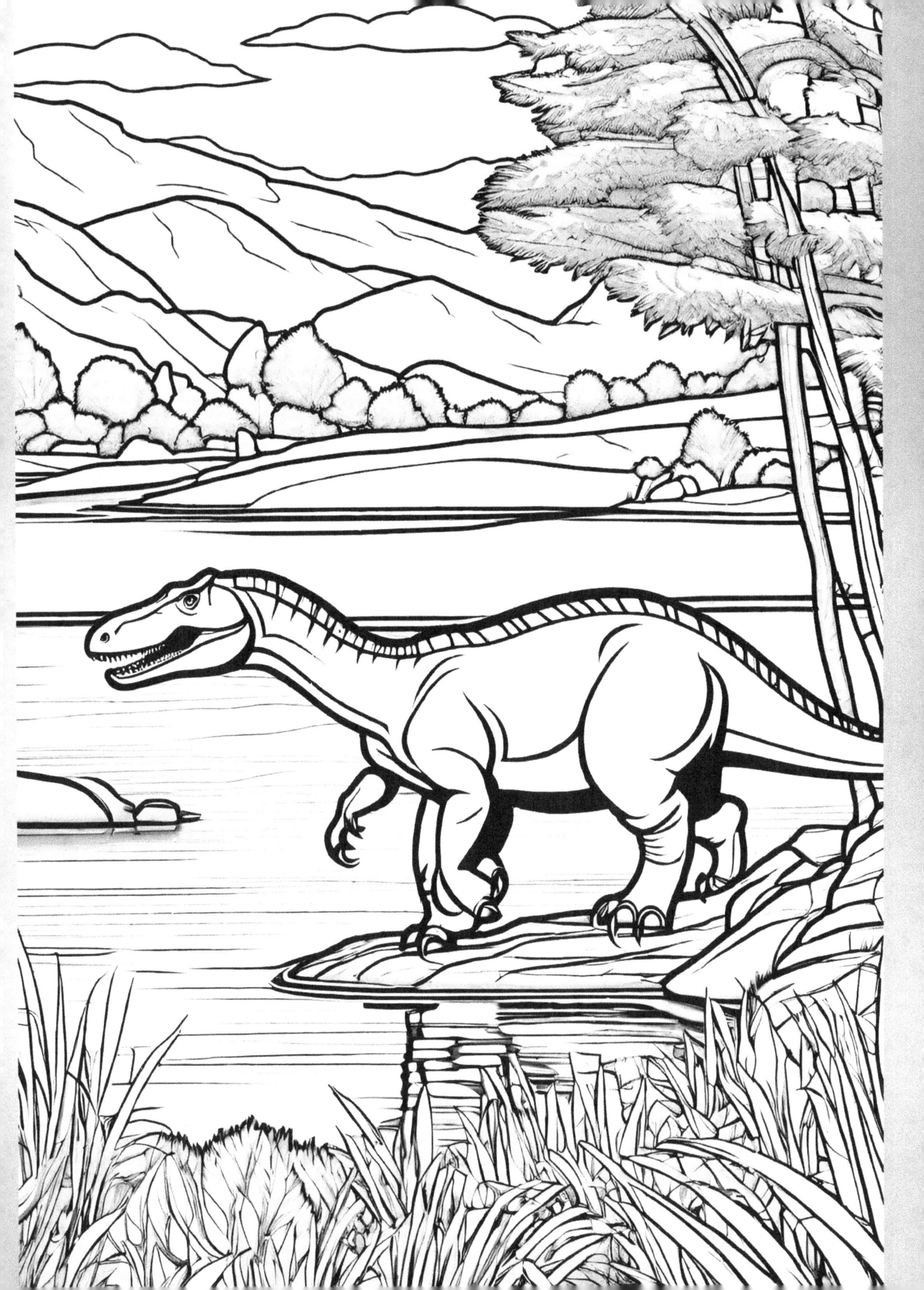

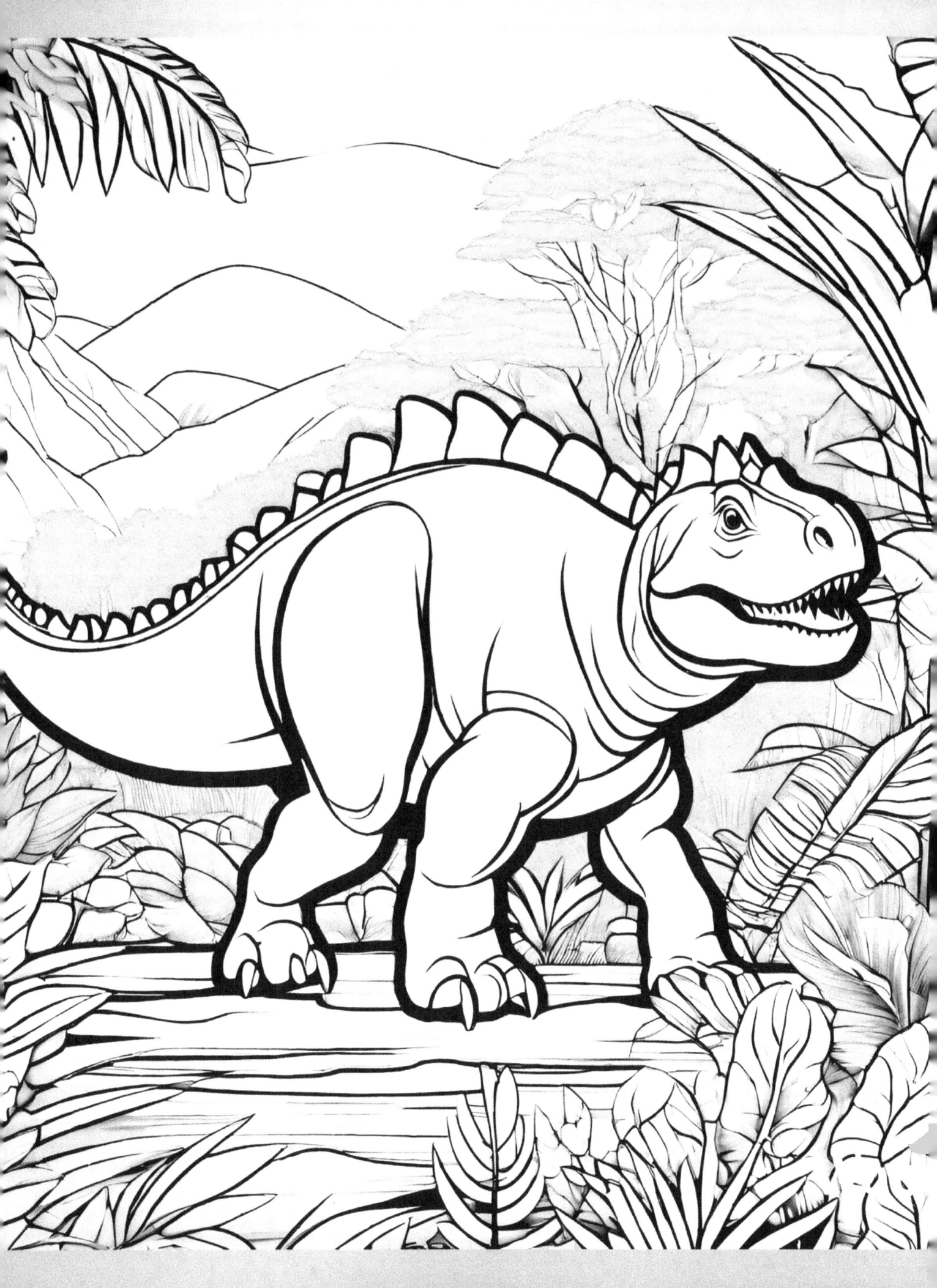

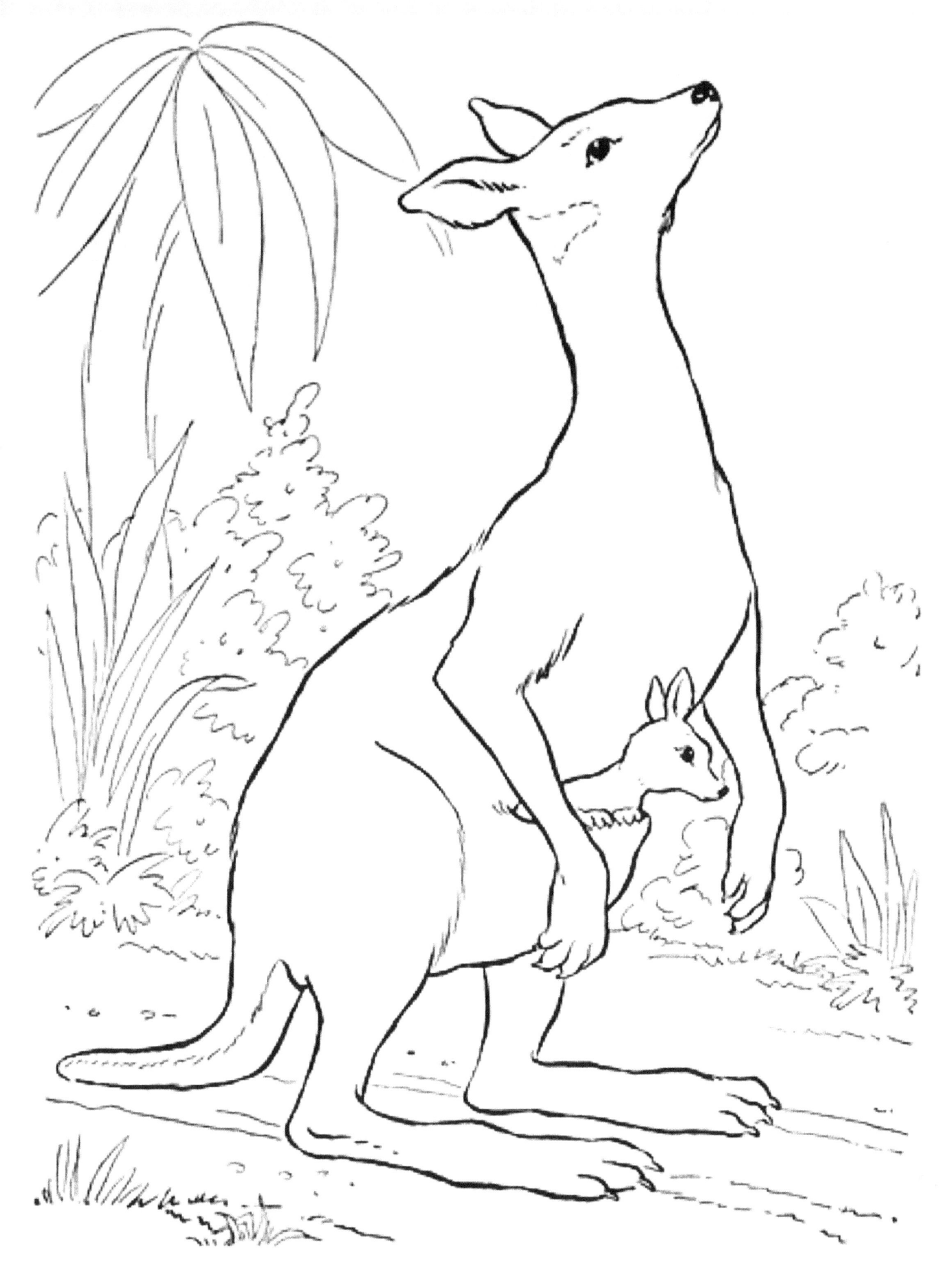

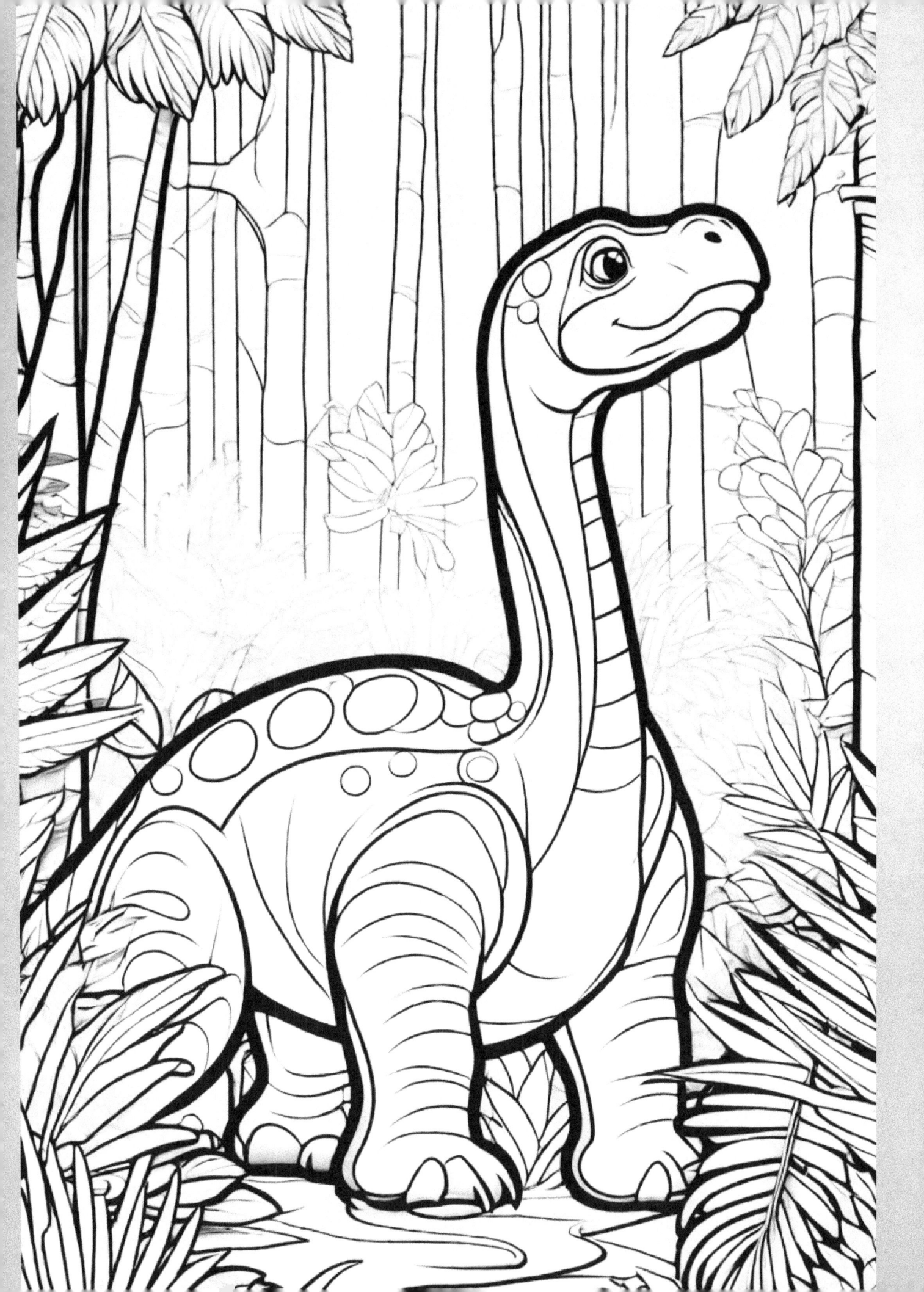

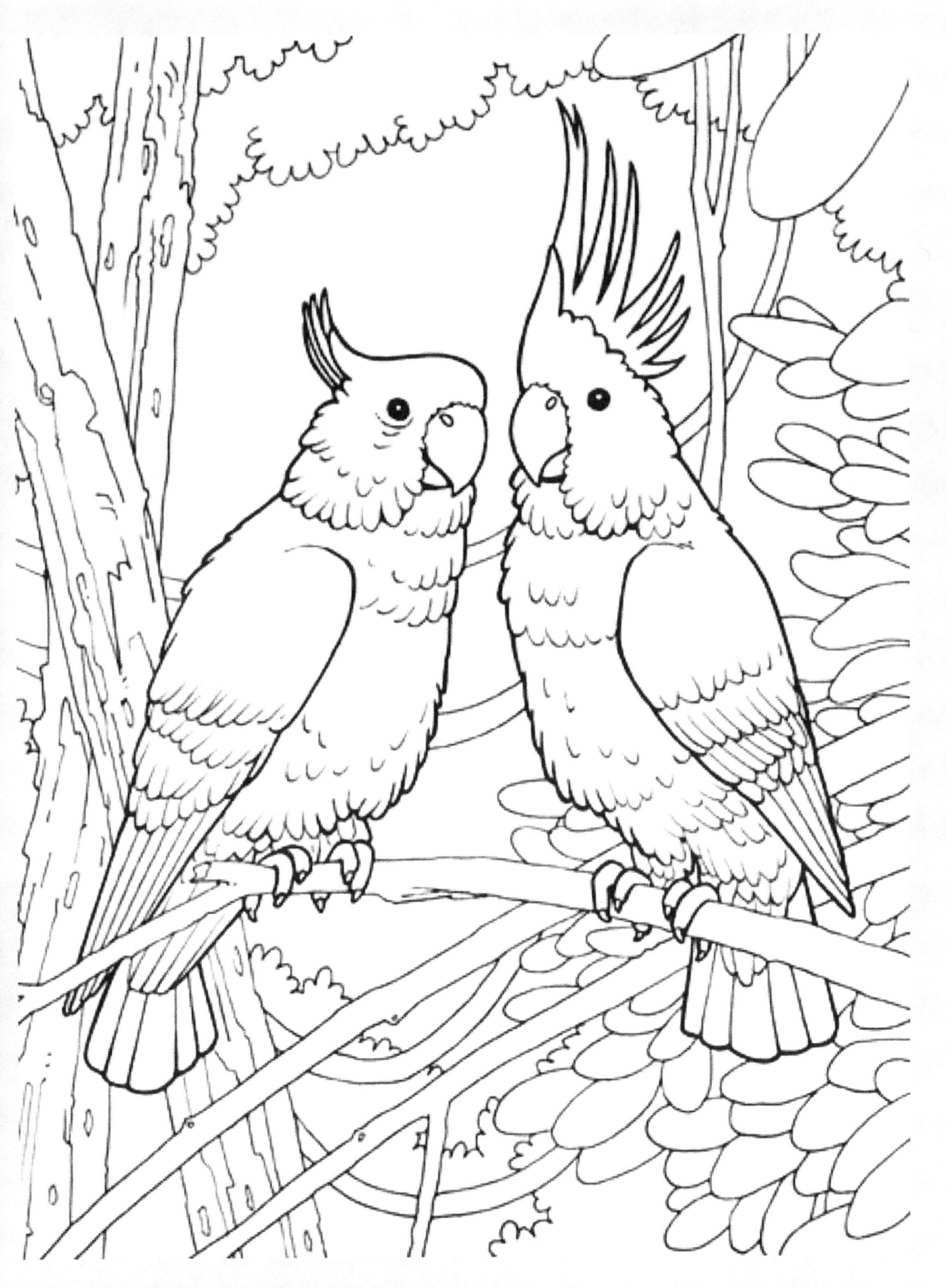

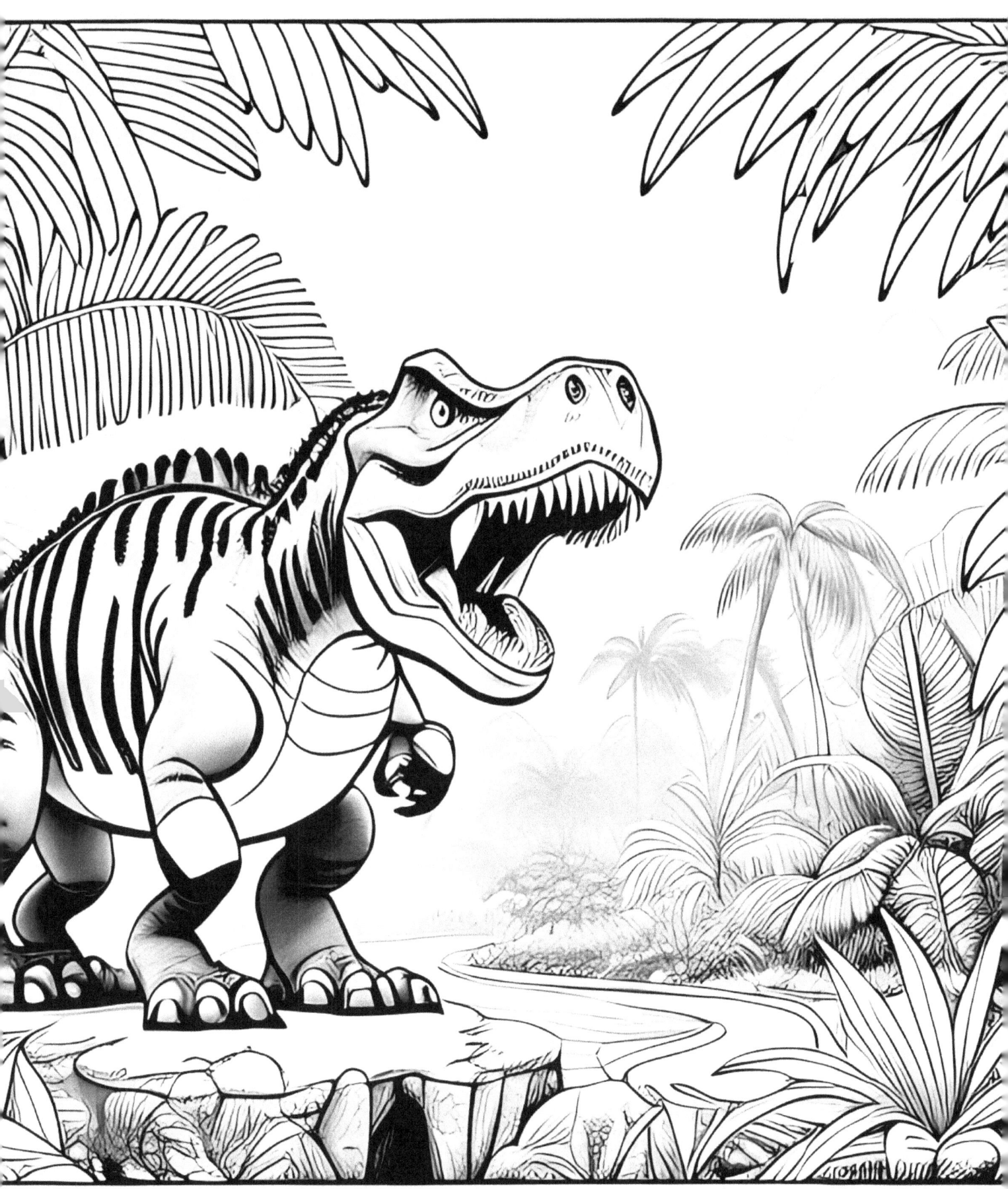

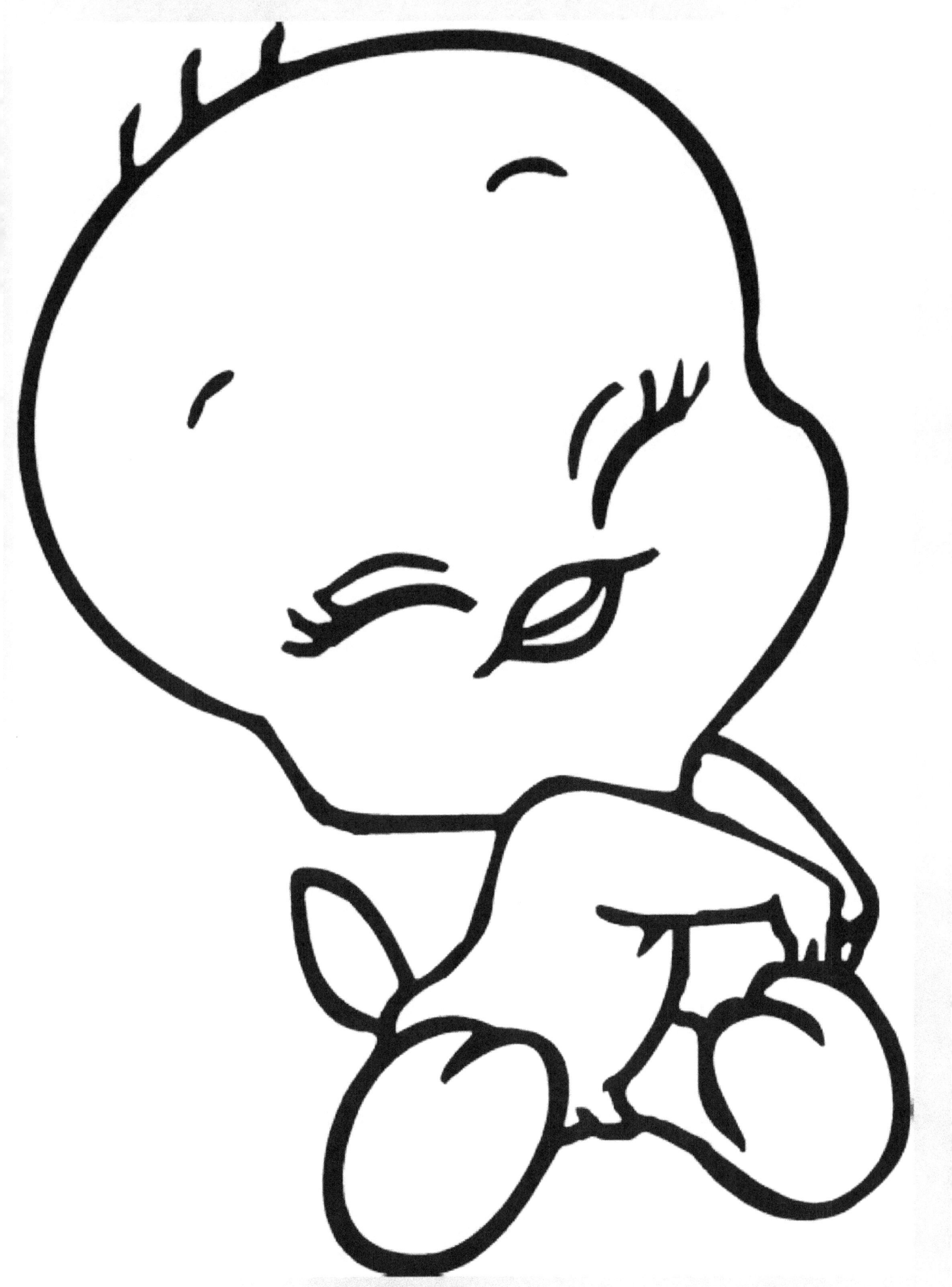

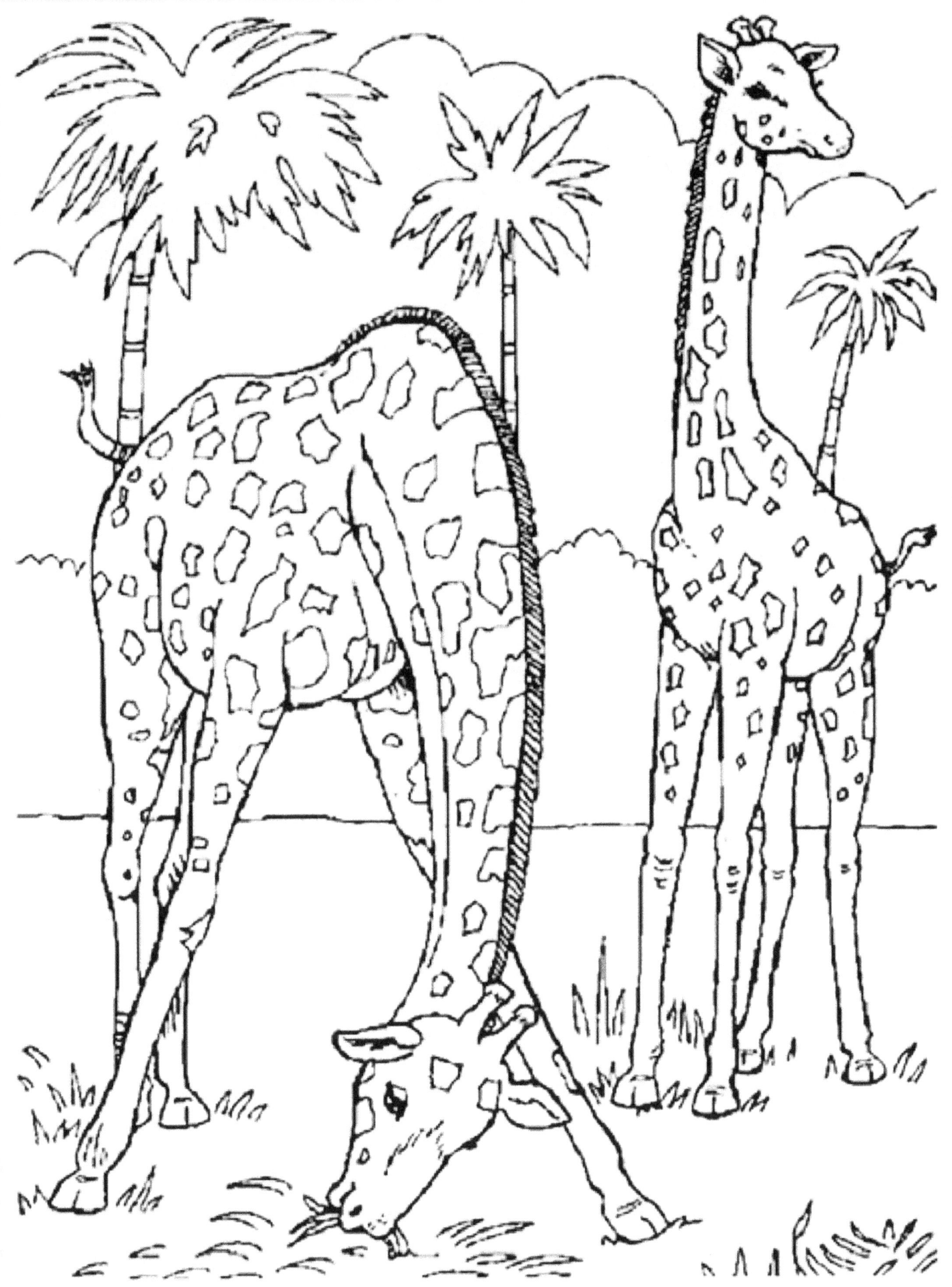

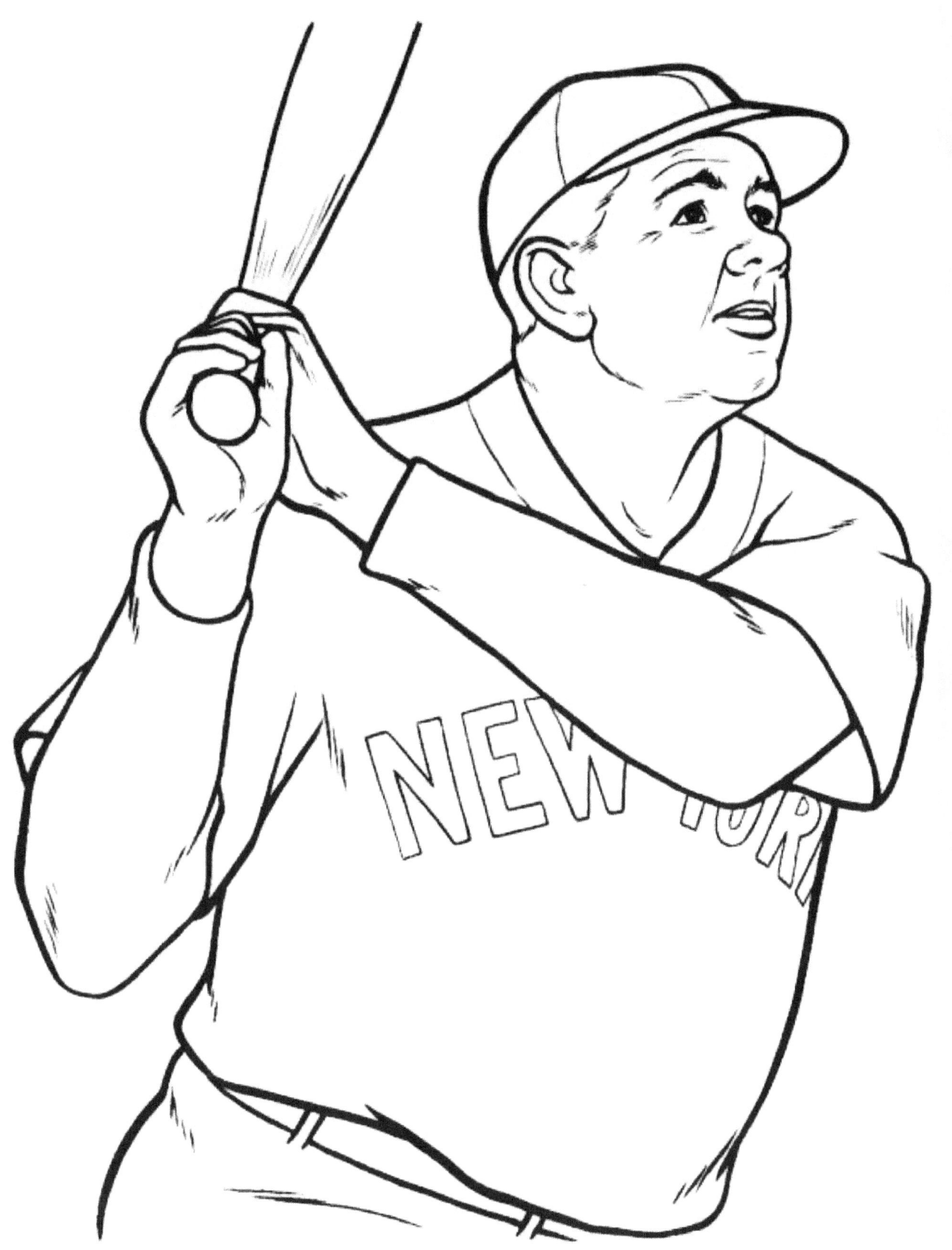

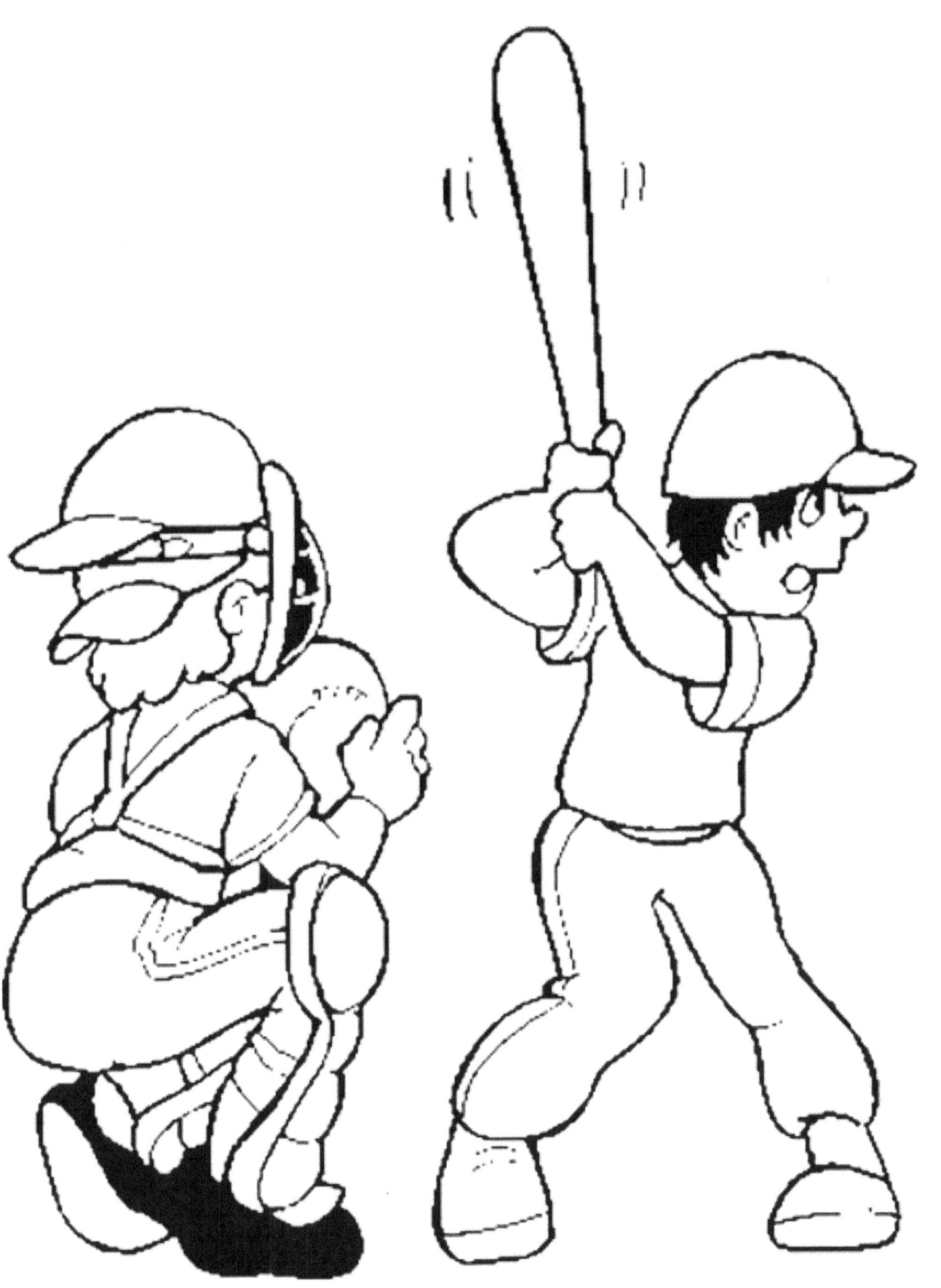

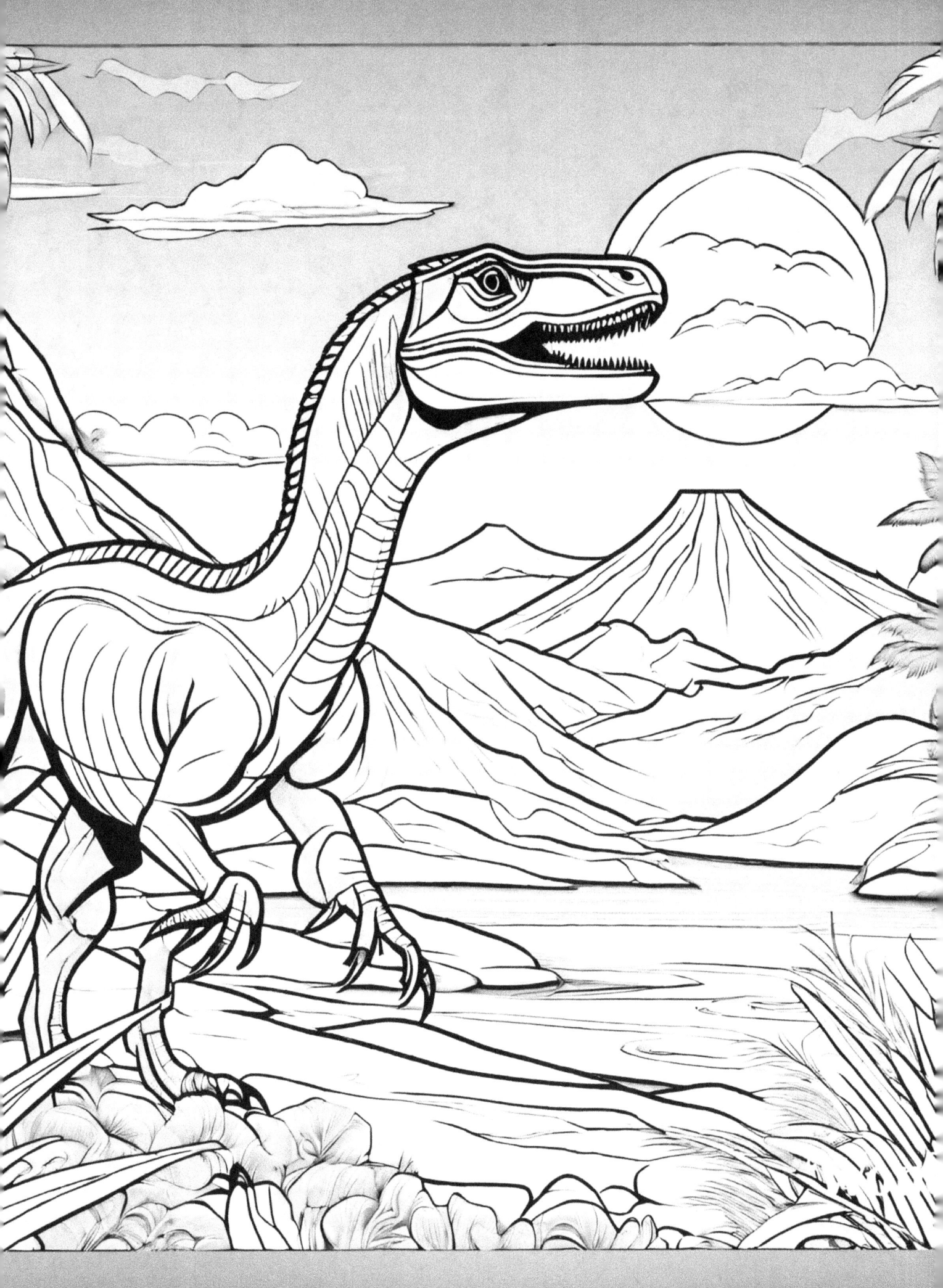

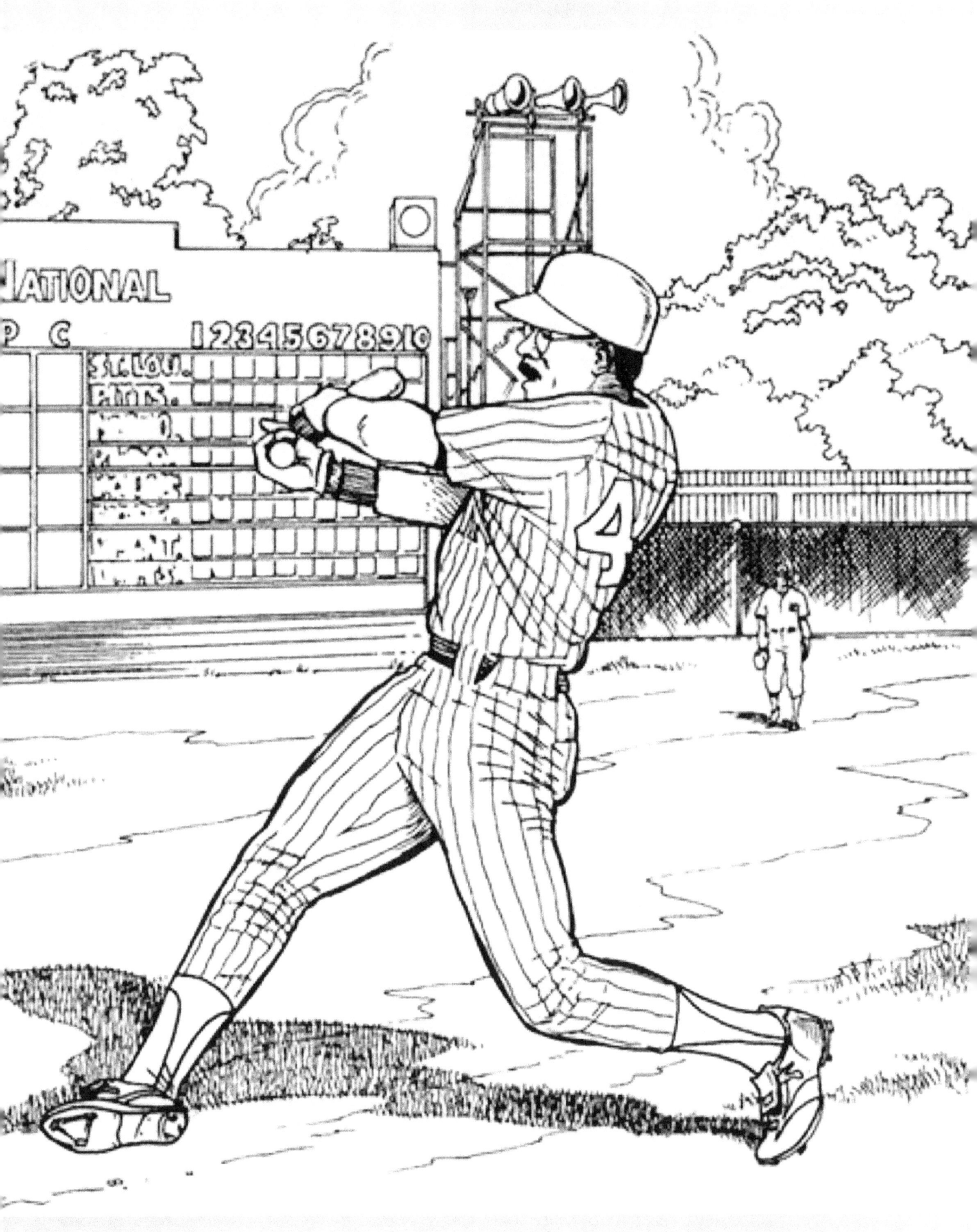

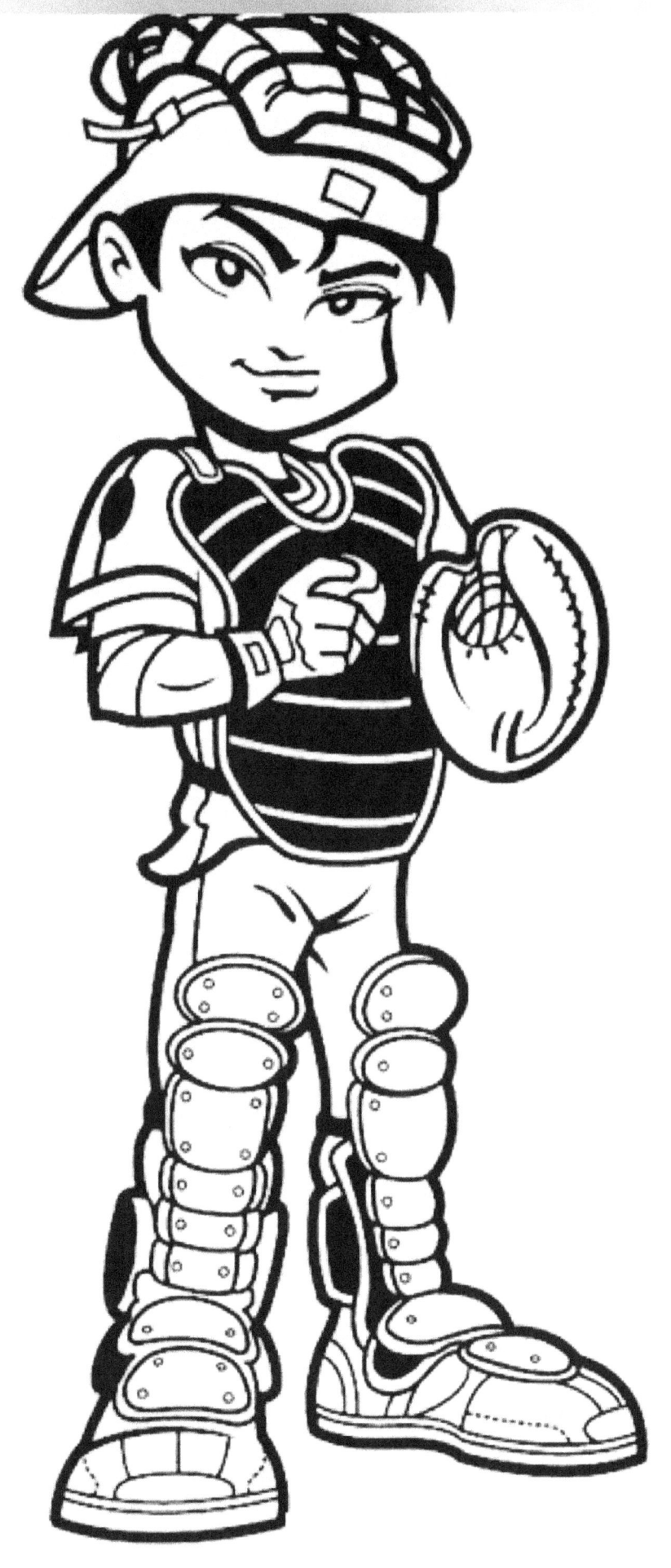

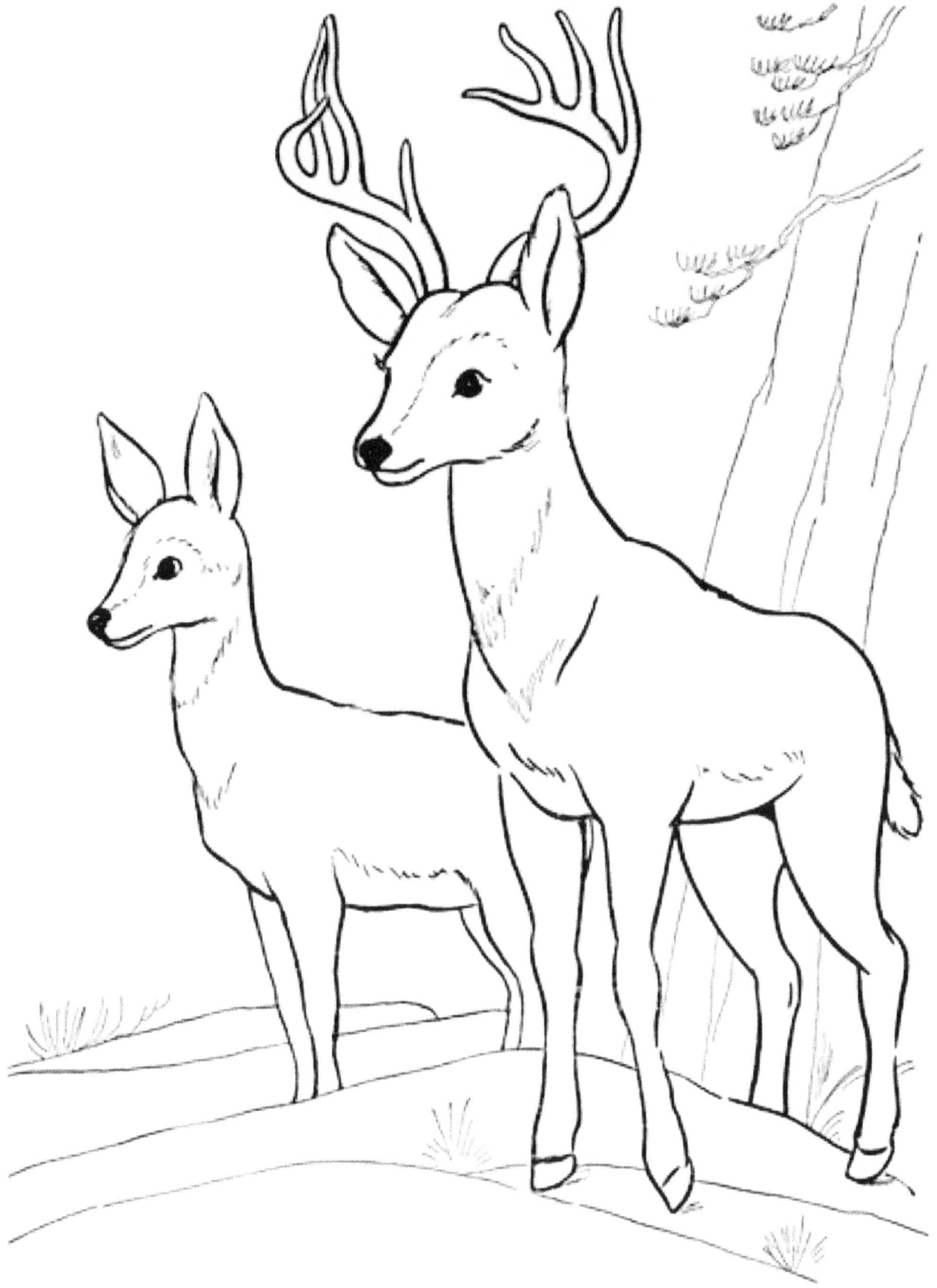

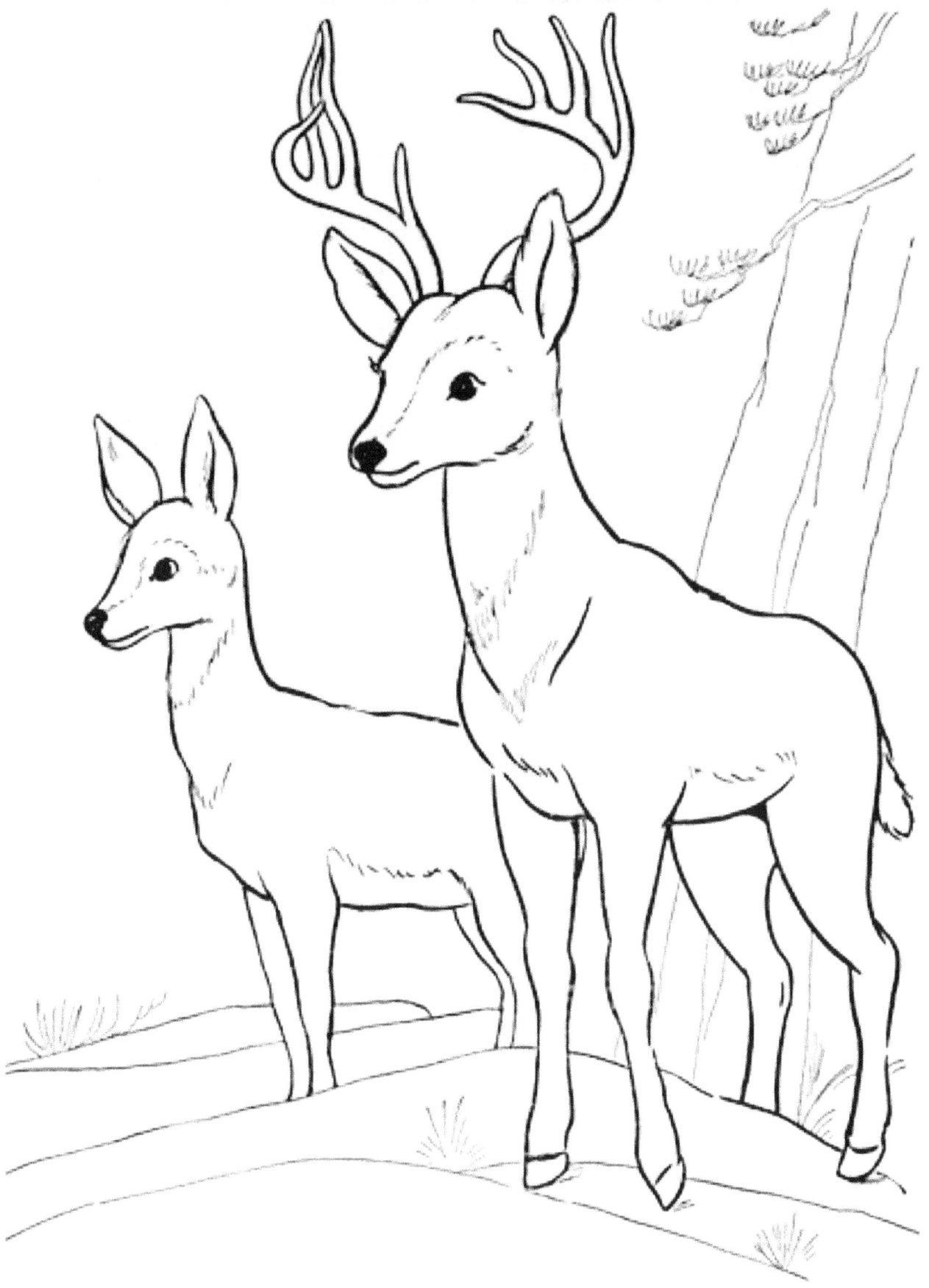

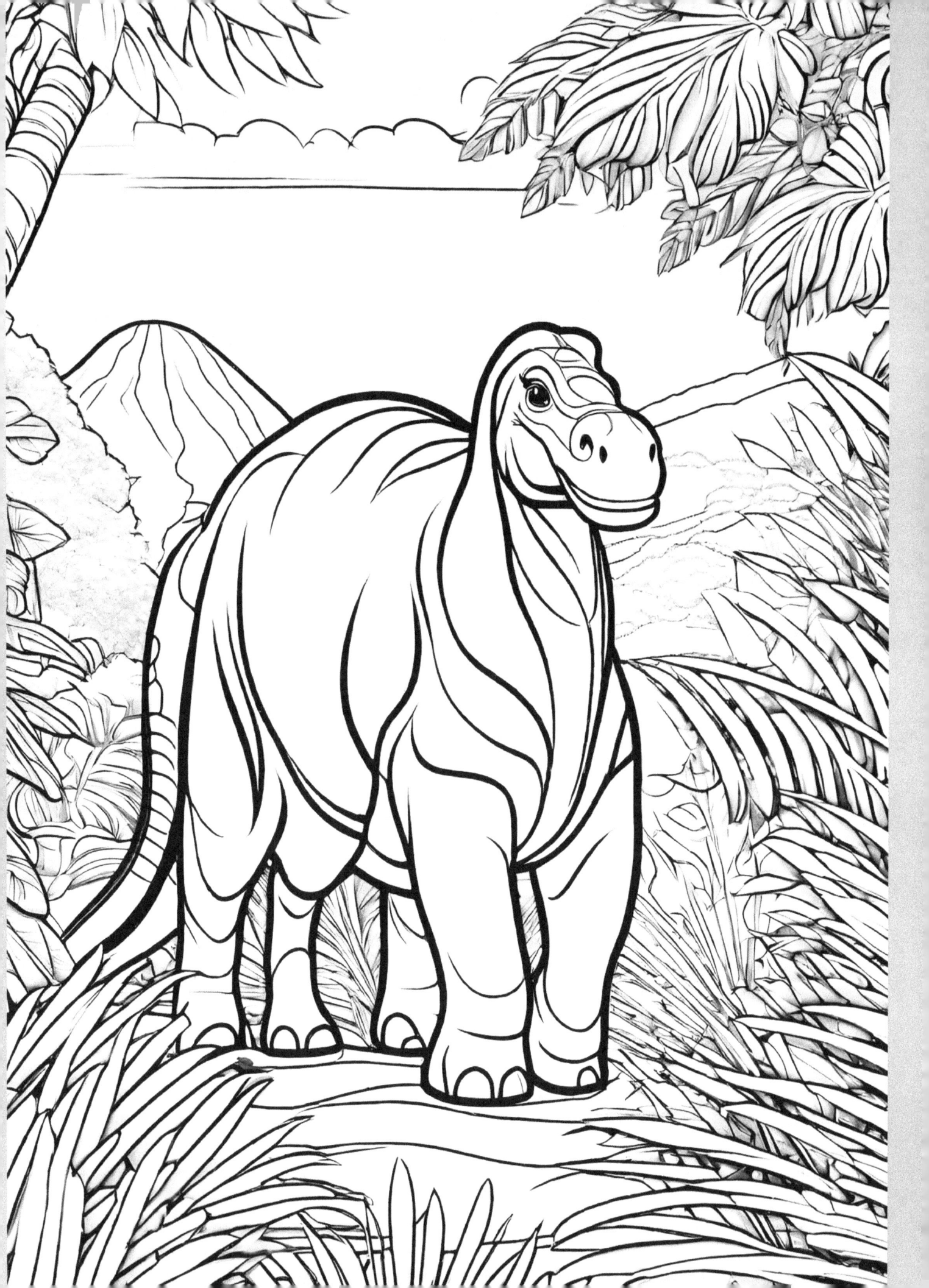

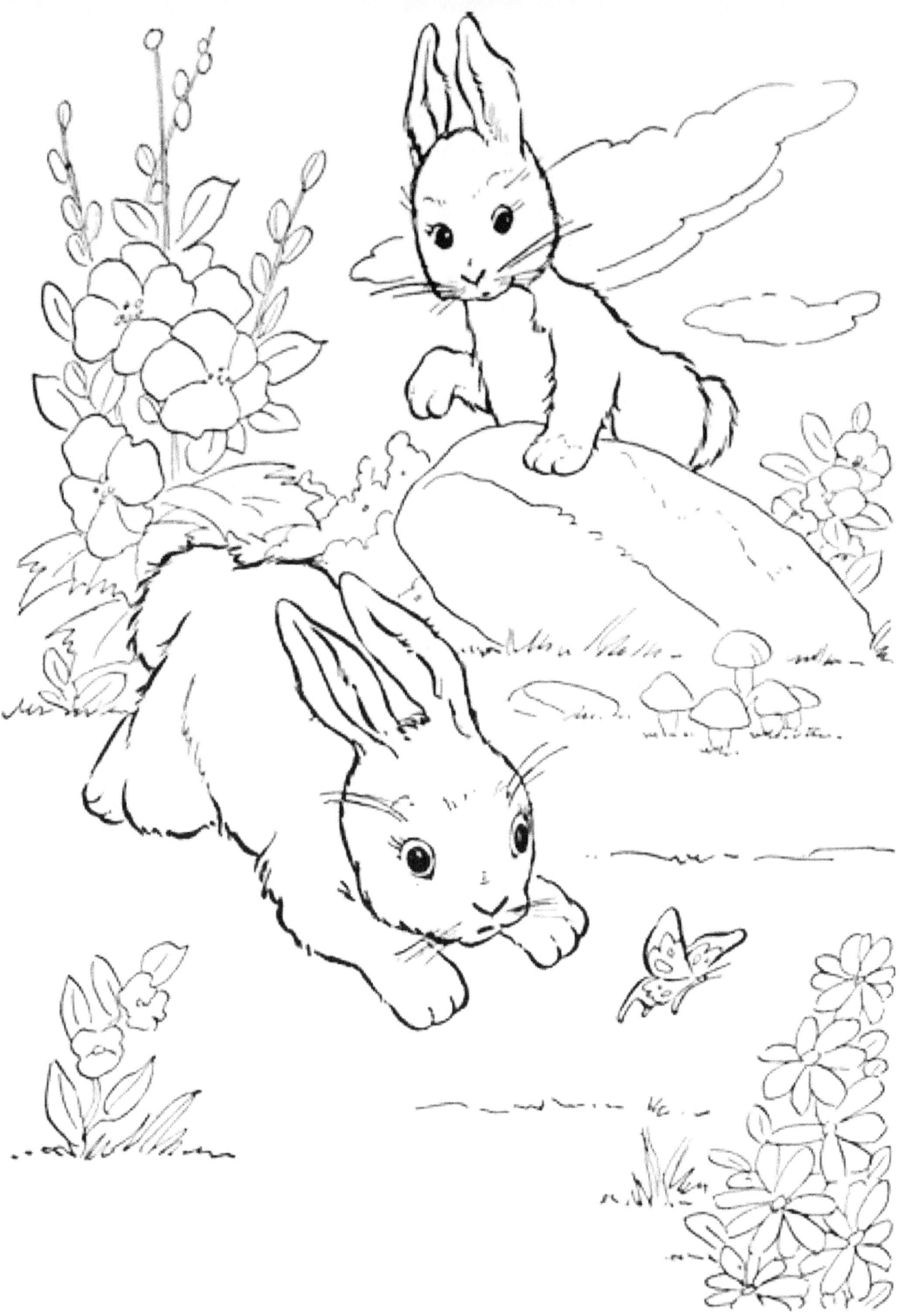

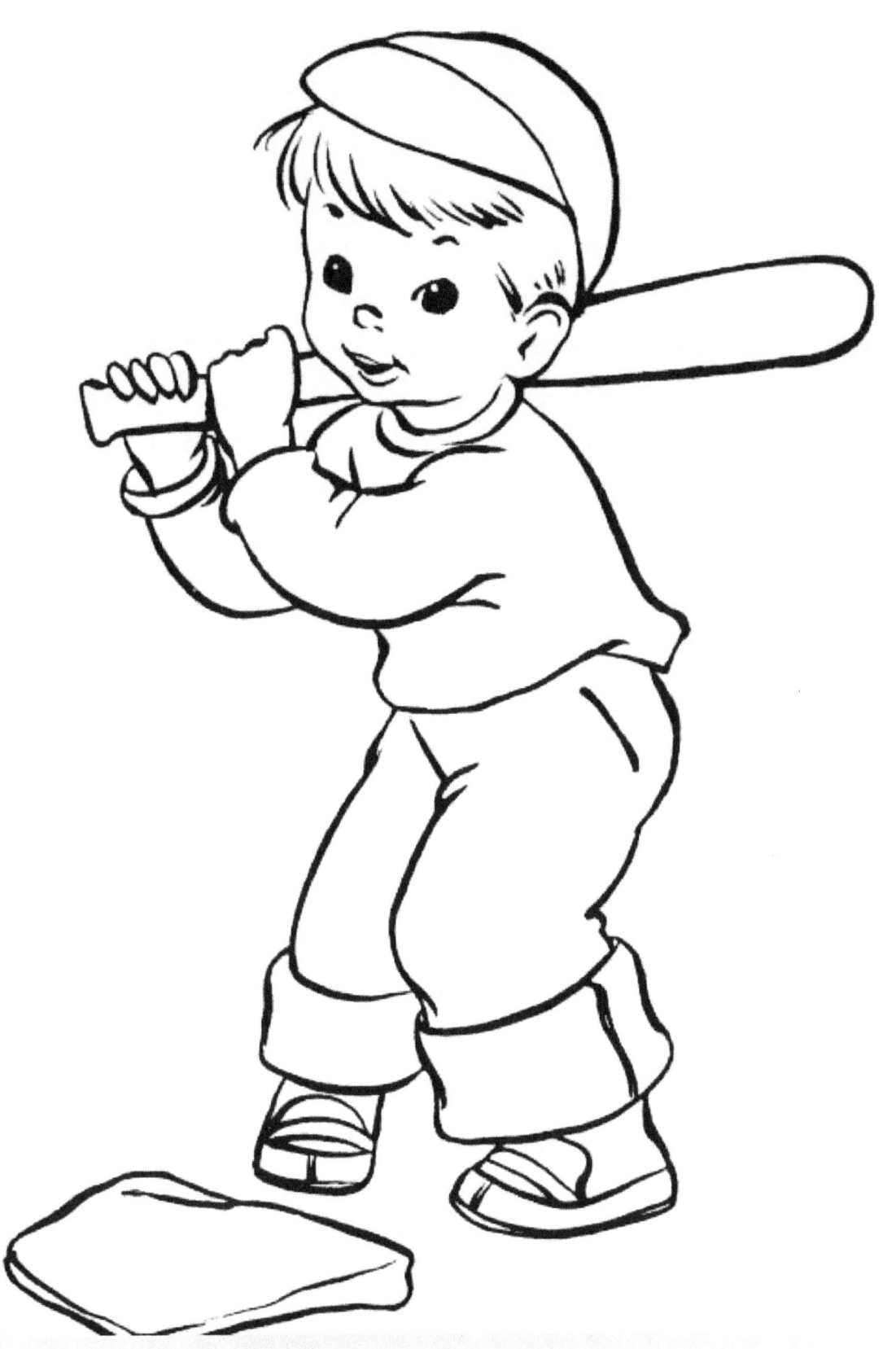

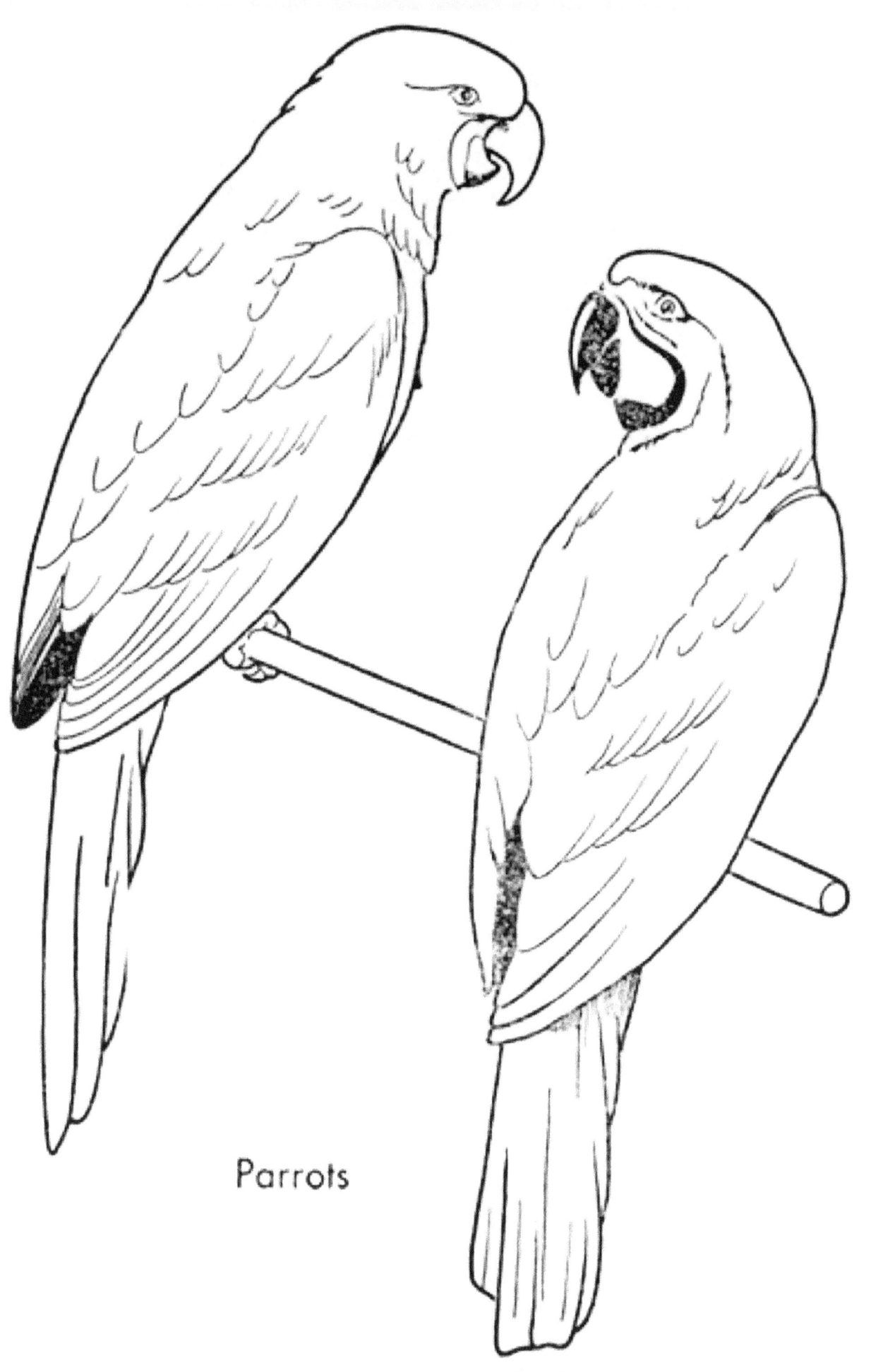

Parrots

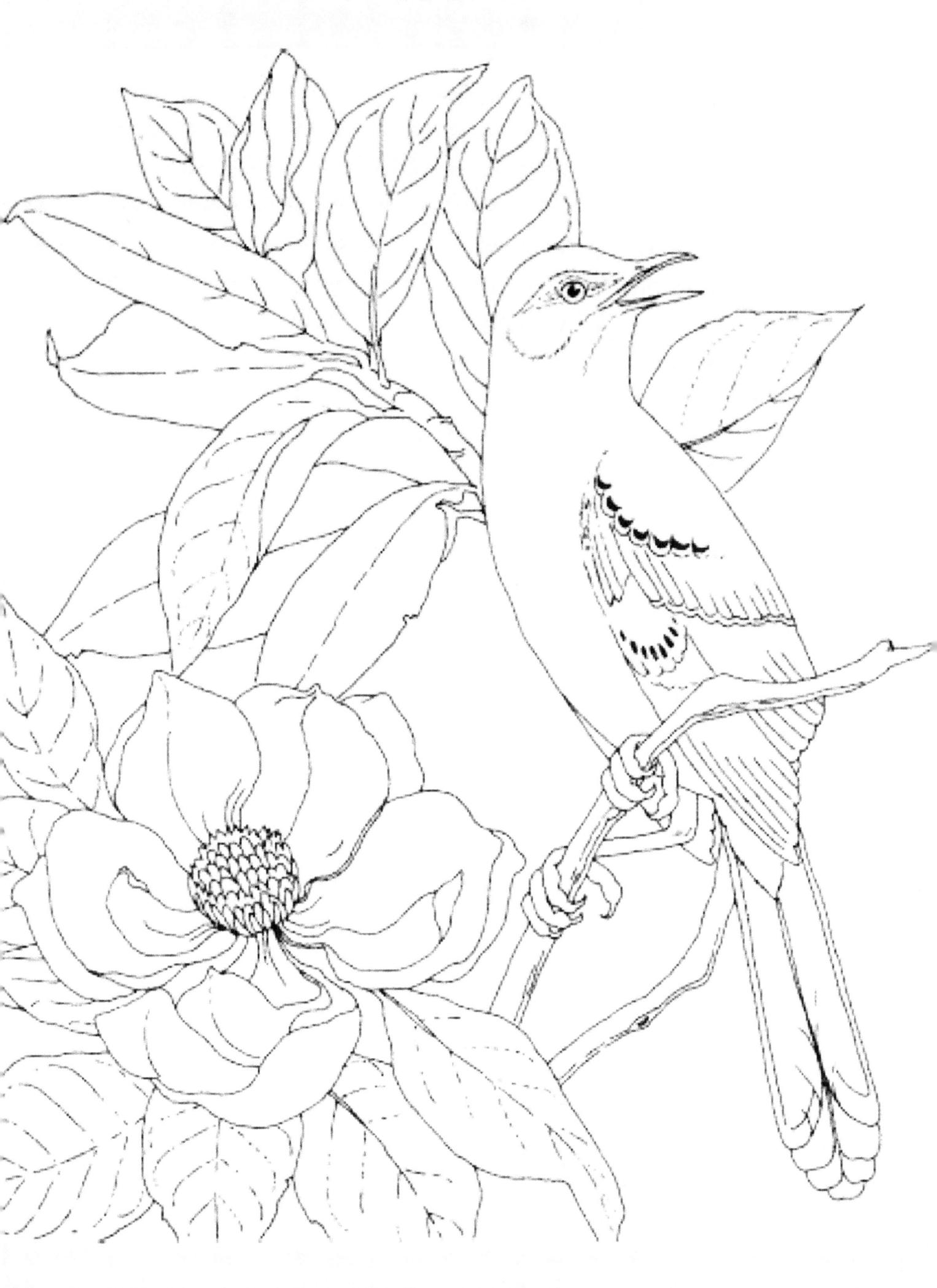

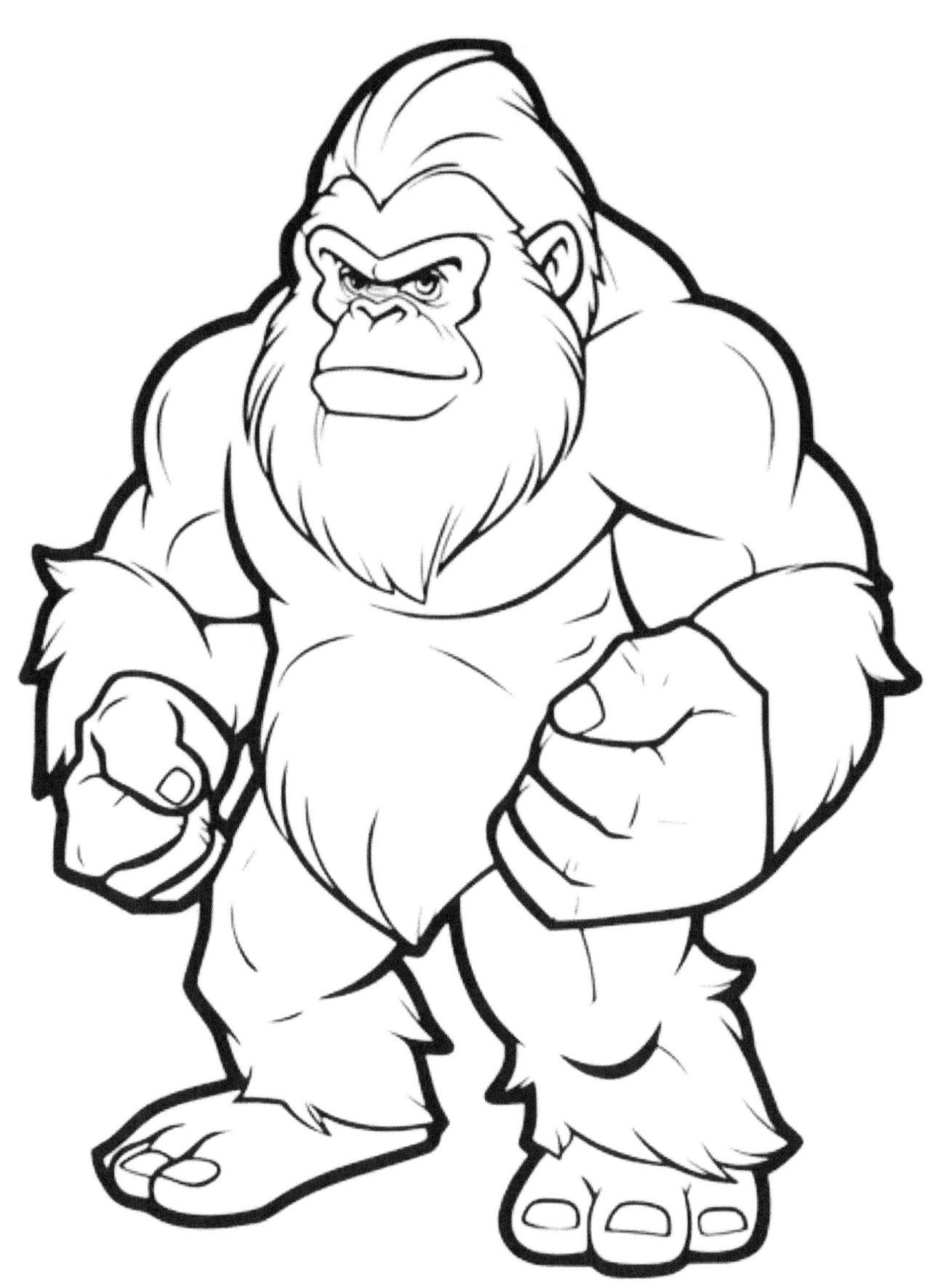

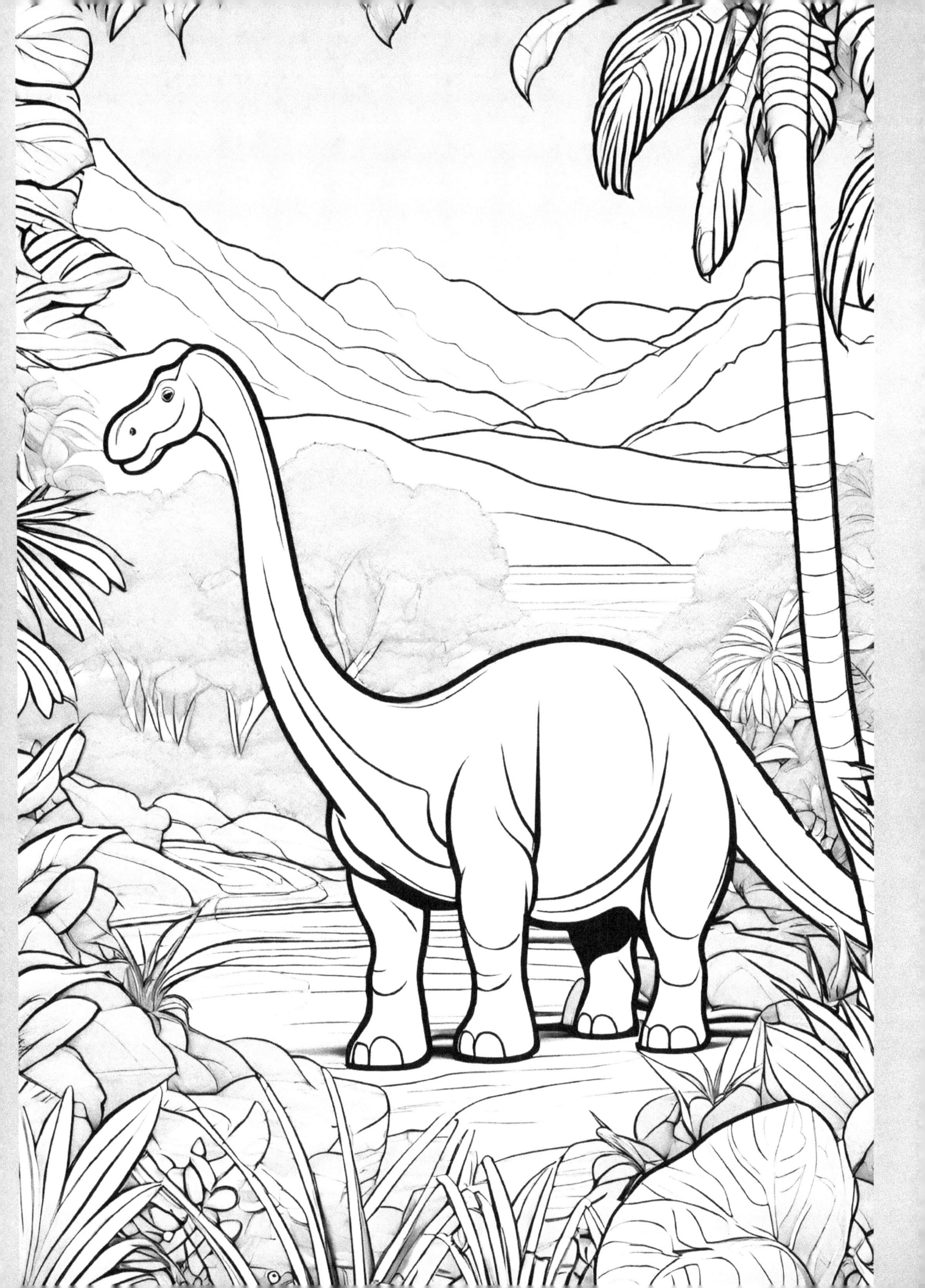

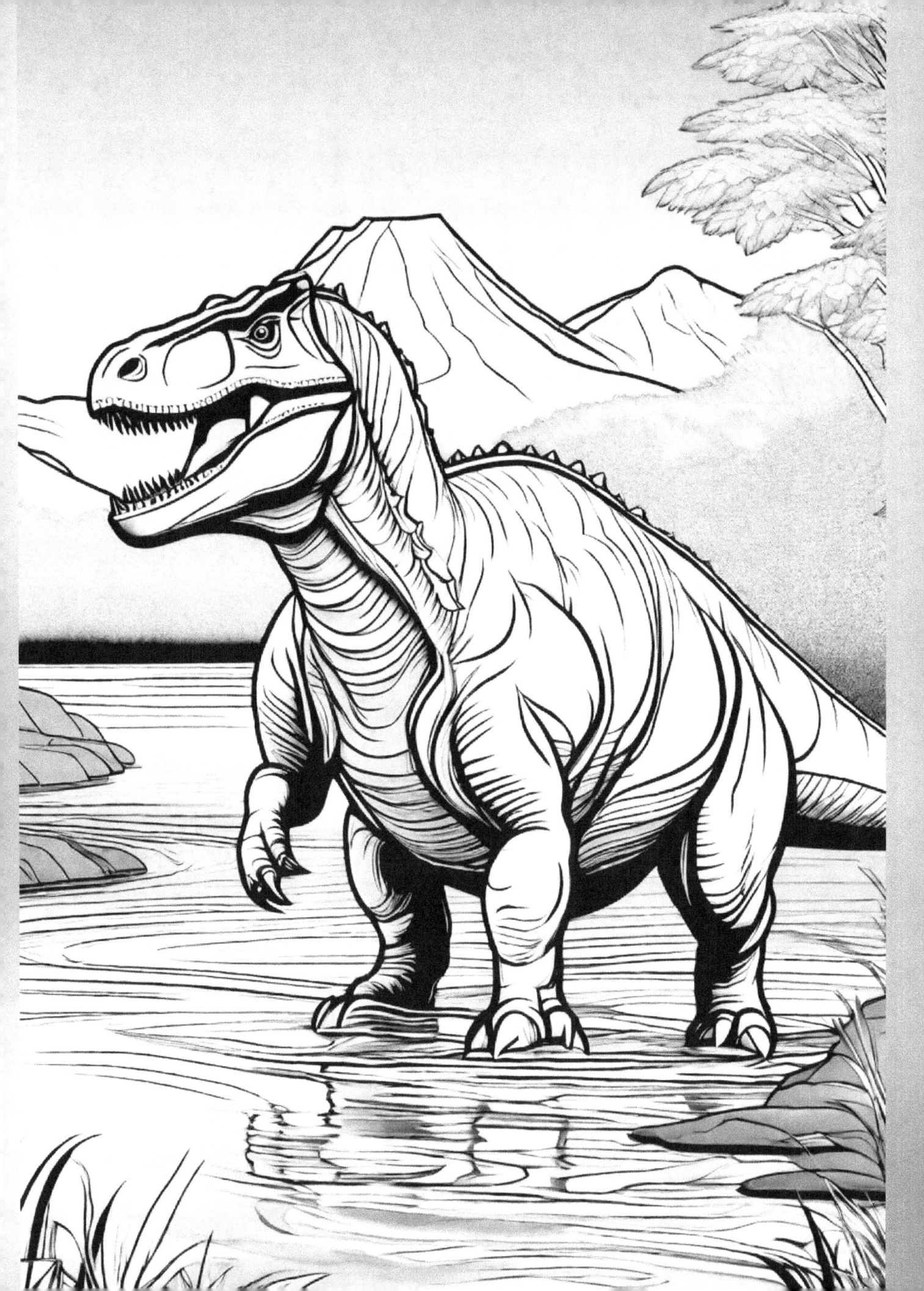

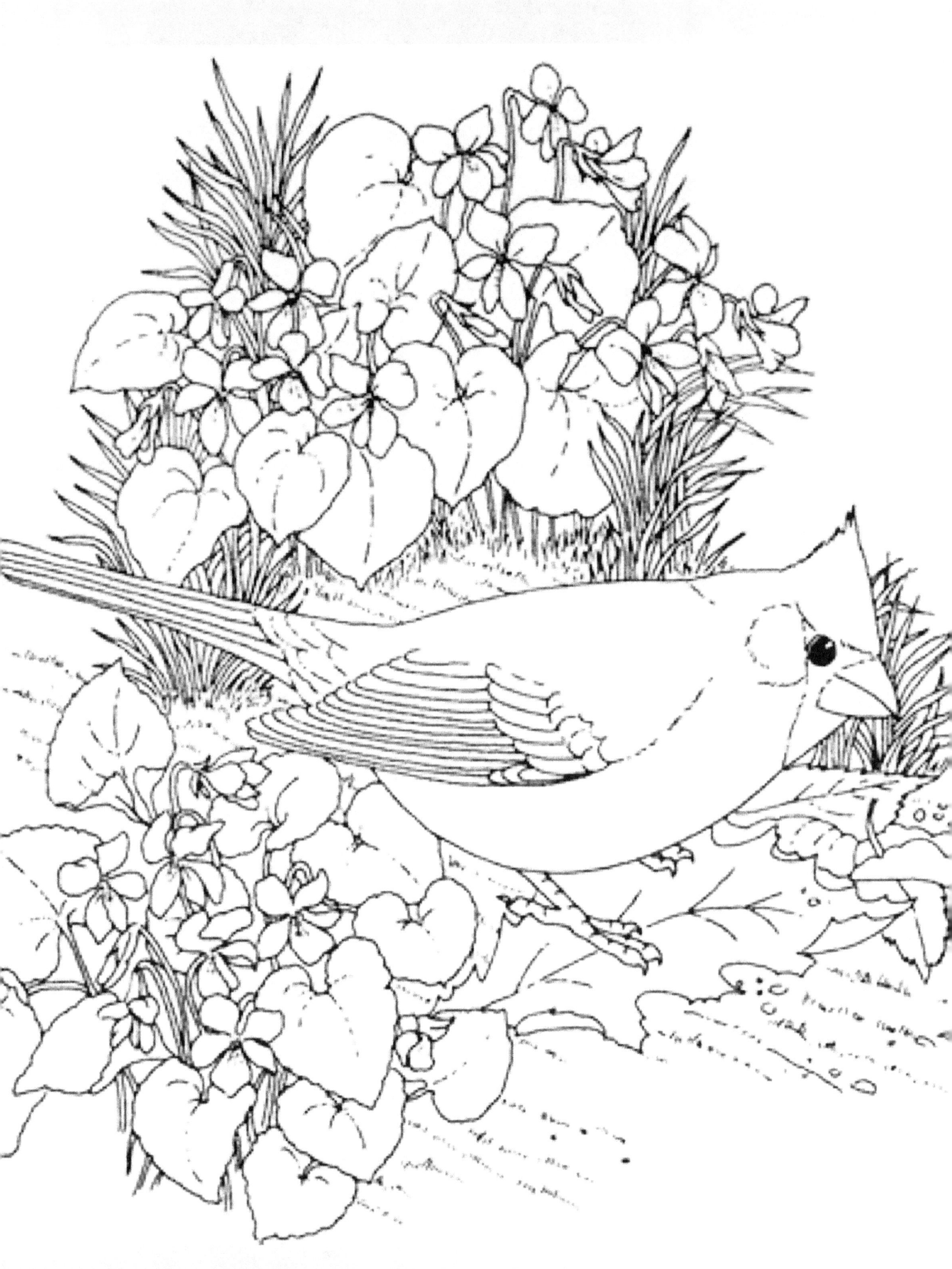

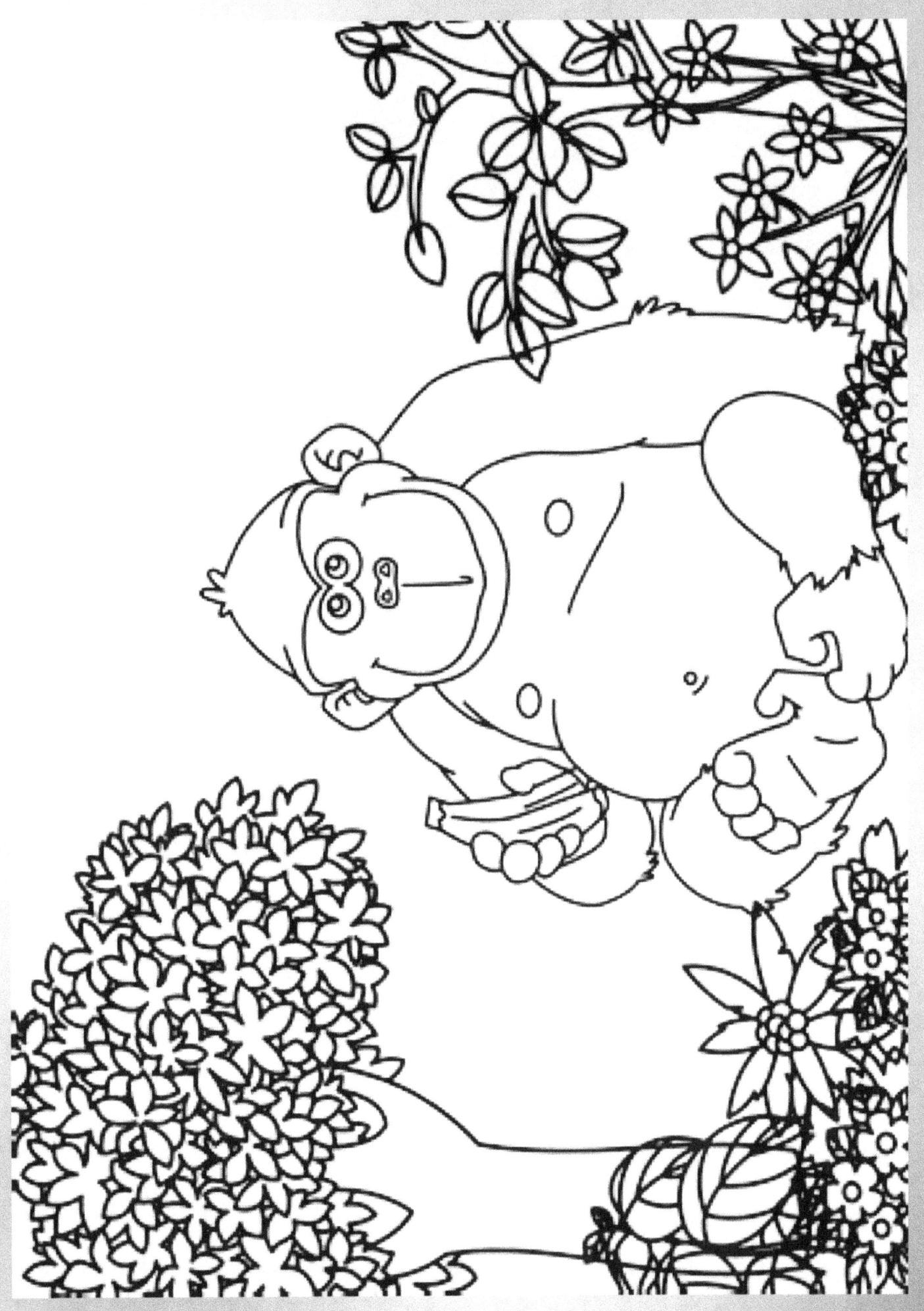

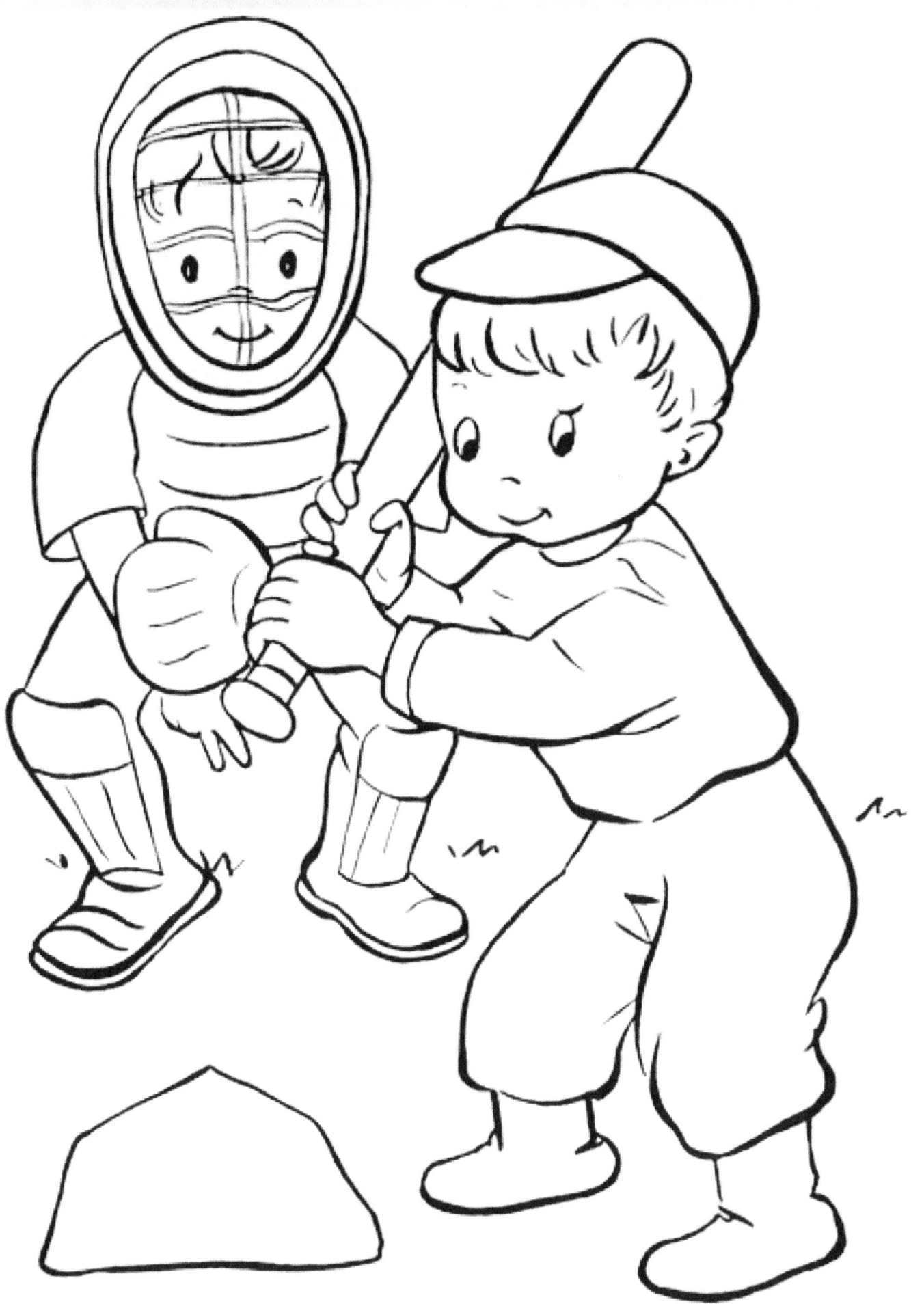

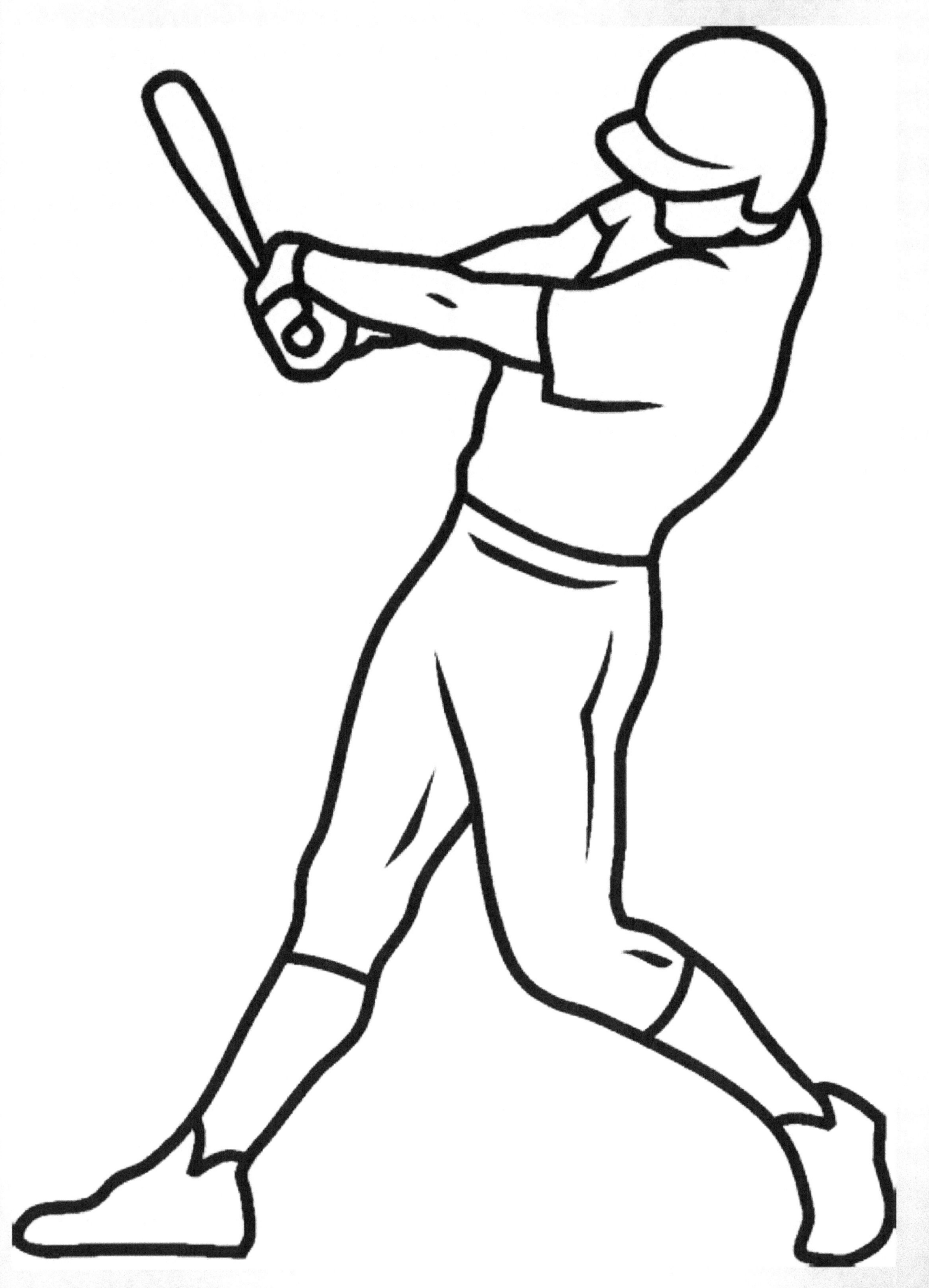

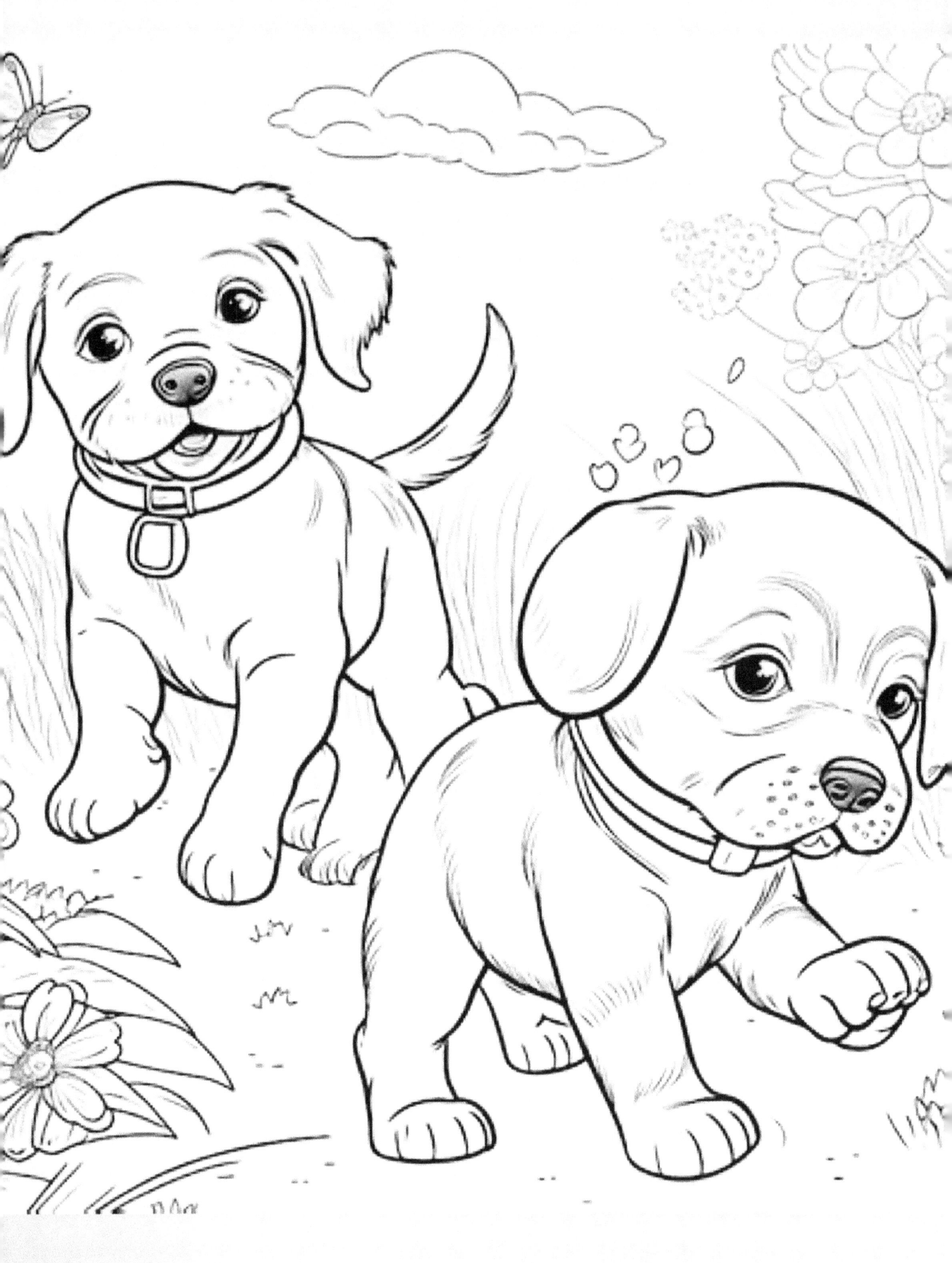

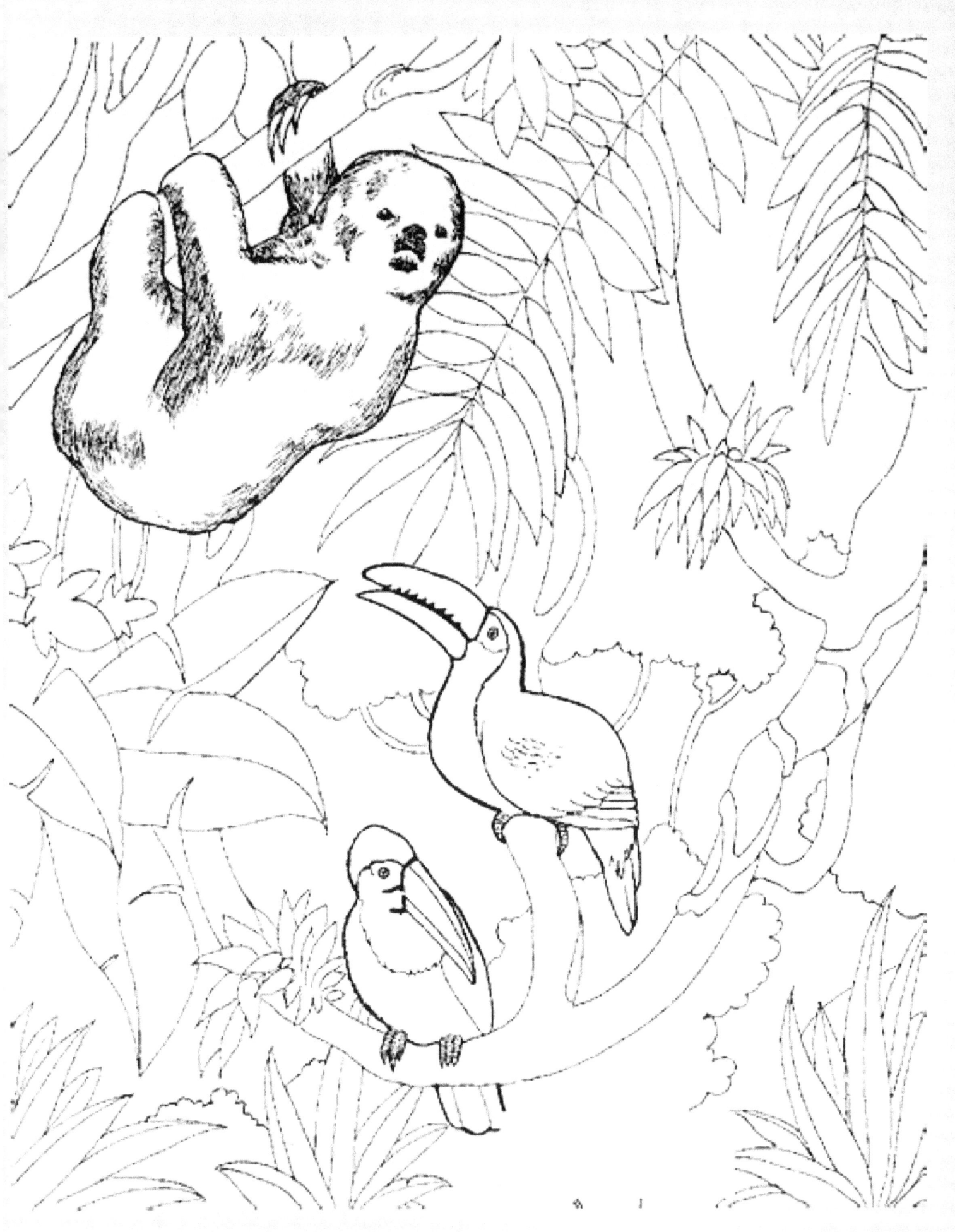

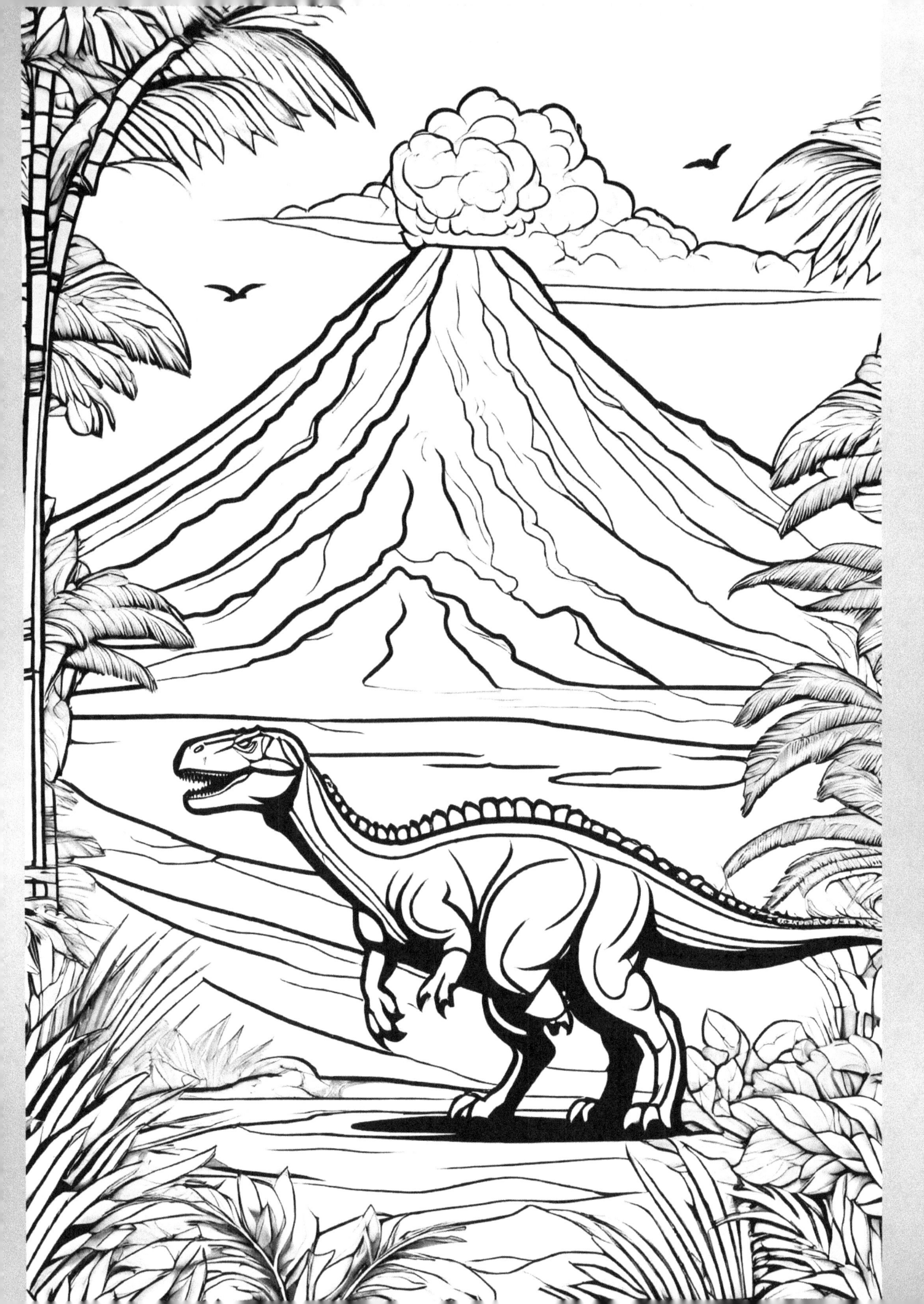

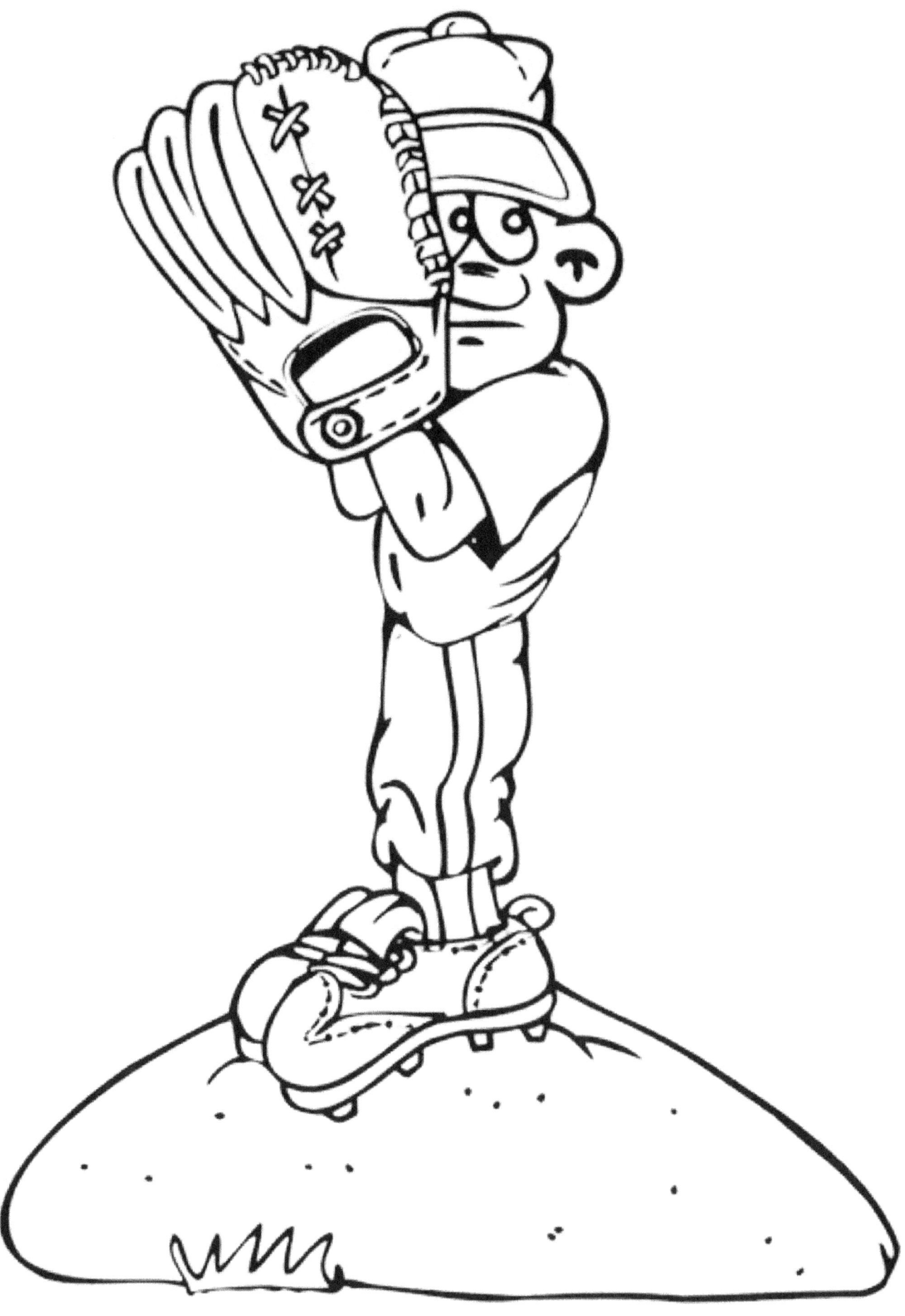

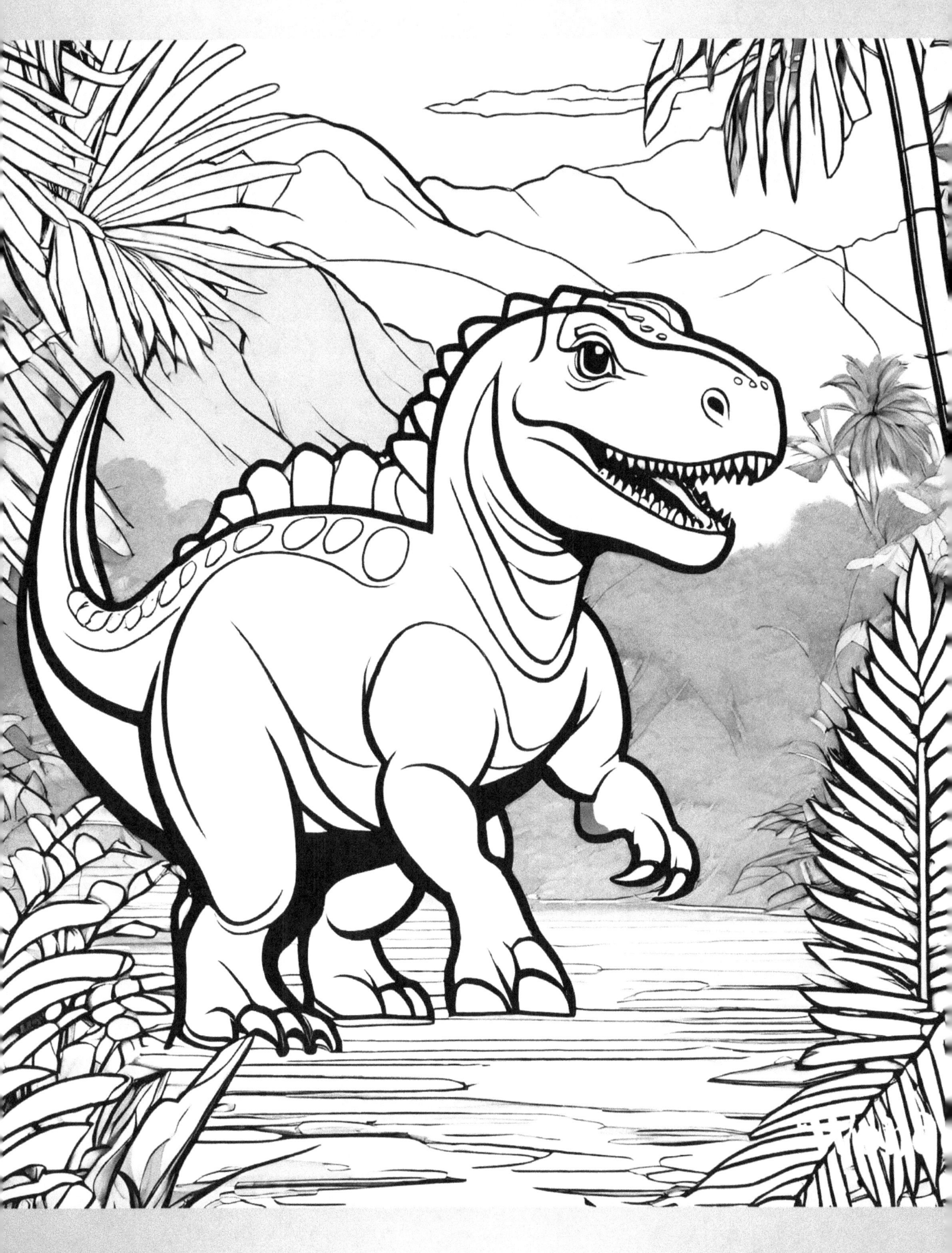

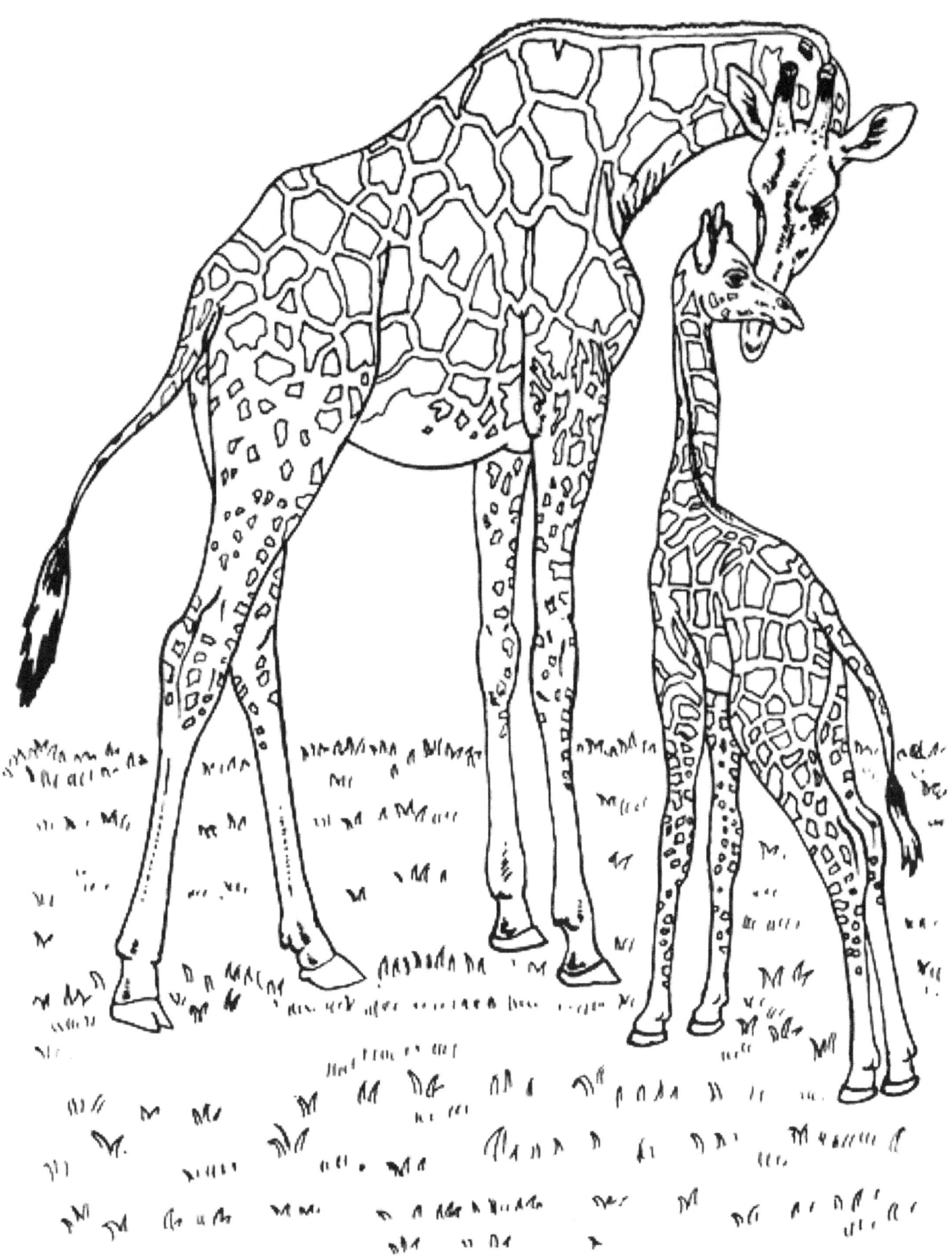

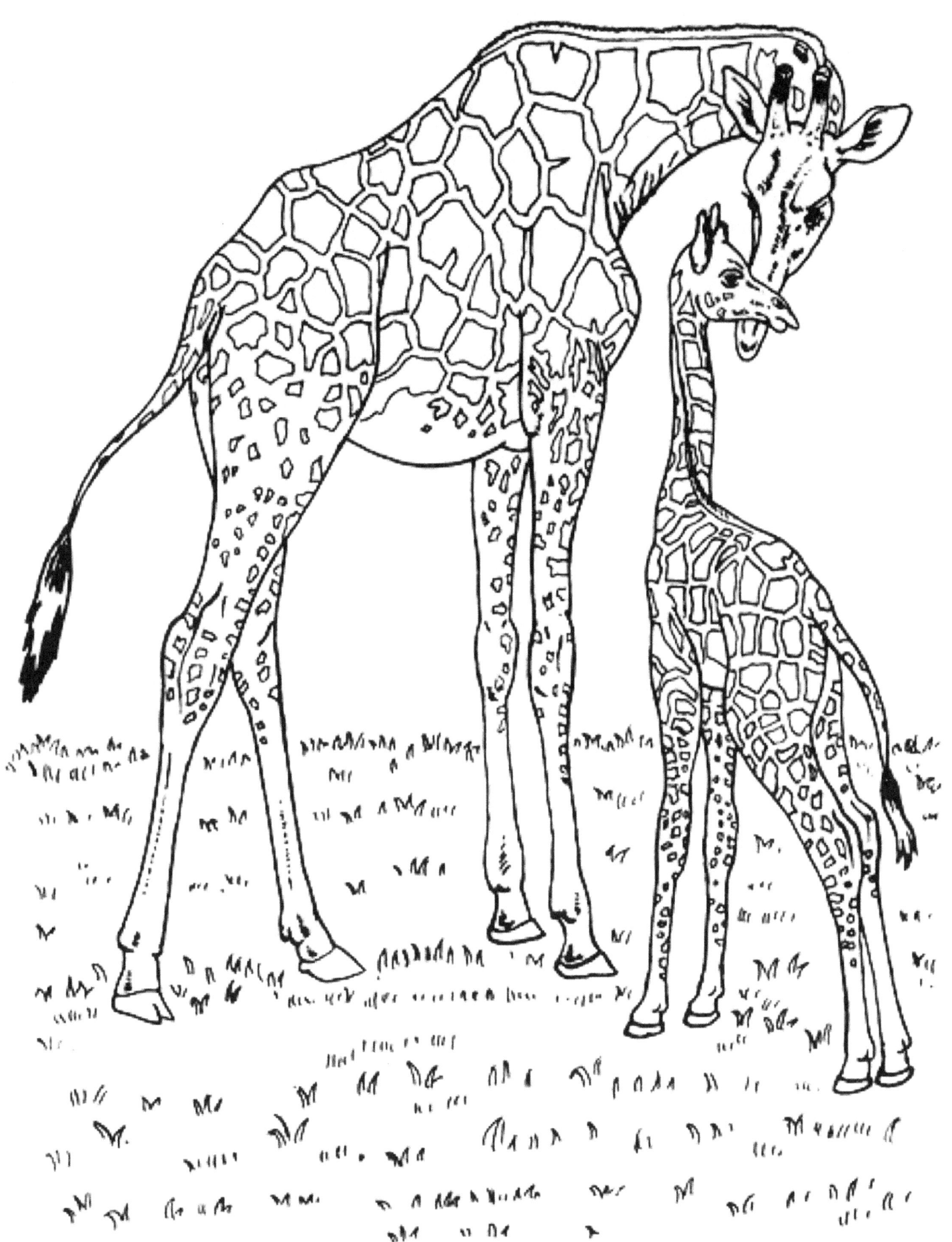

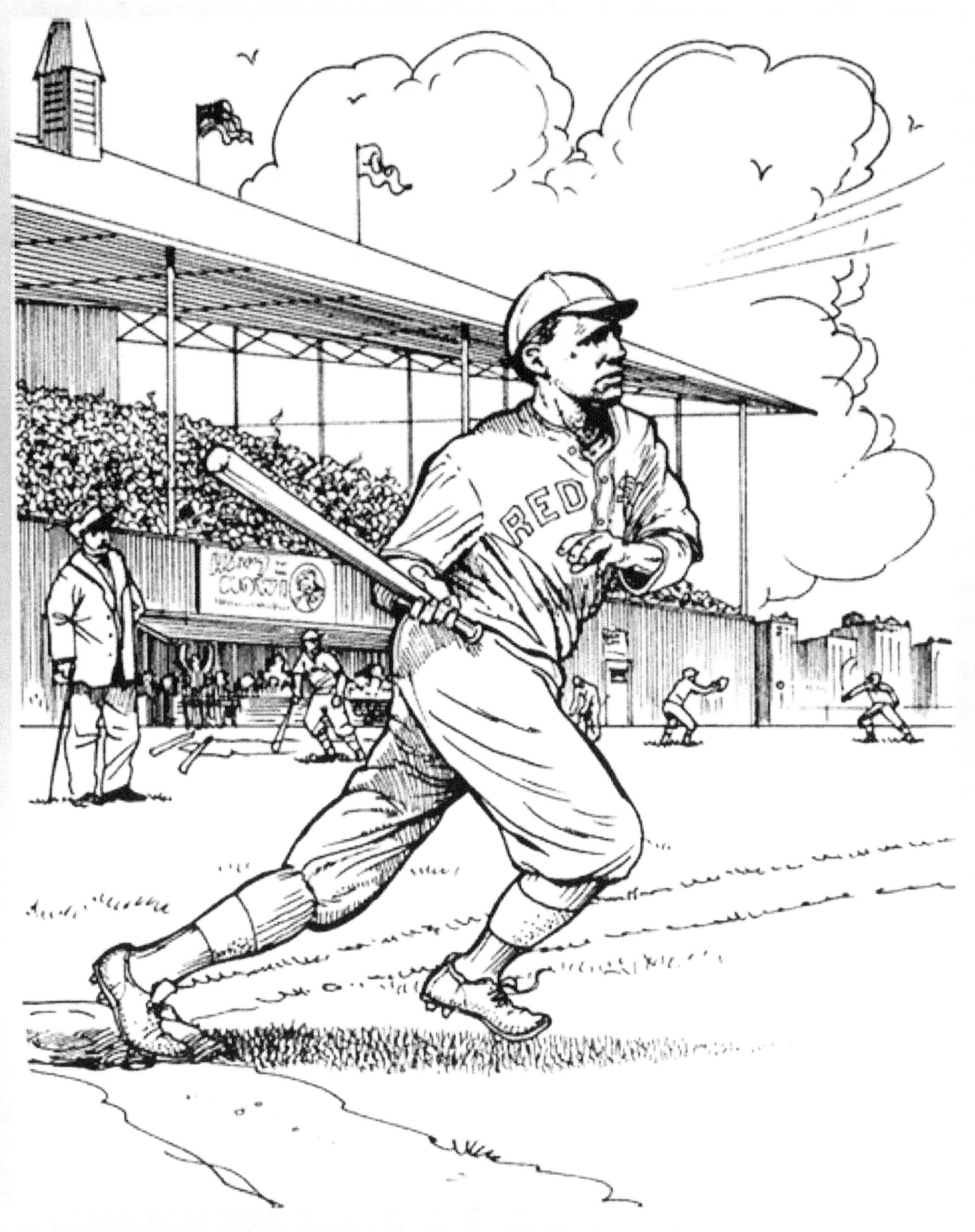

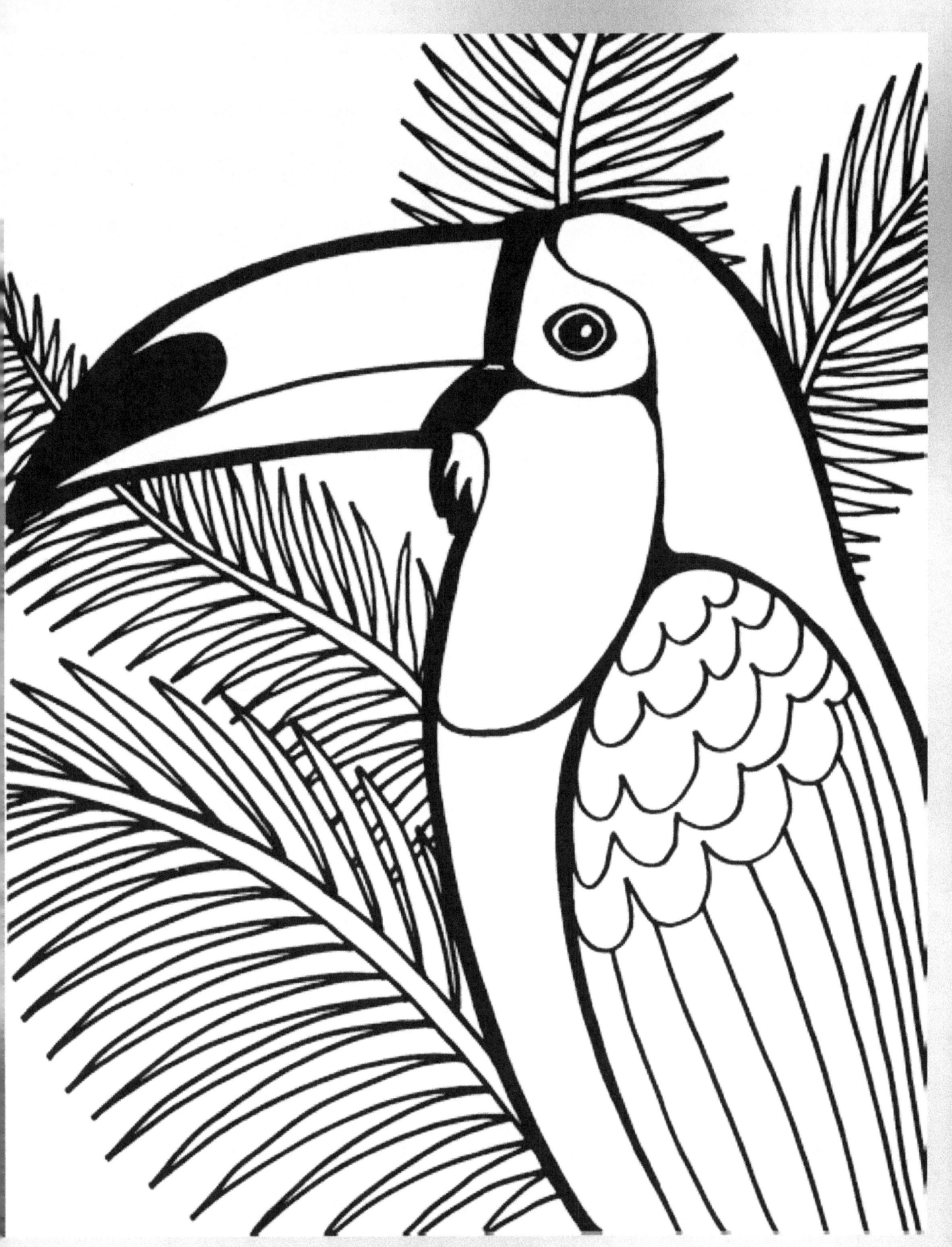

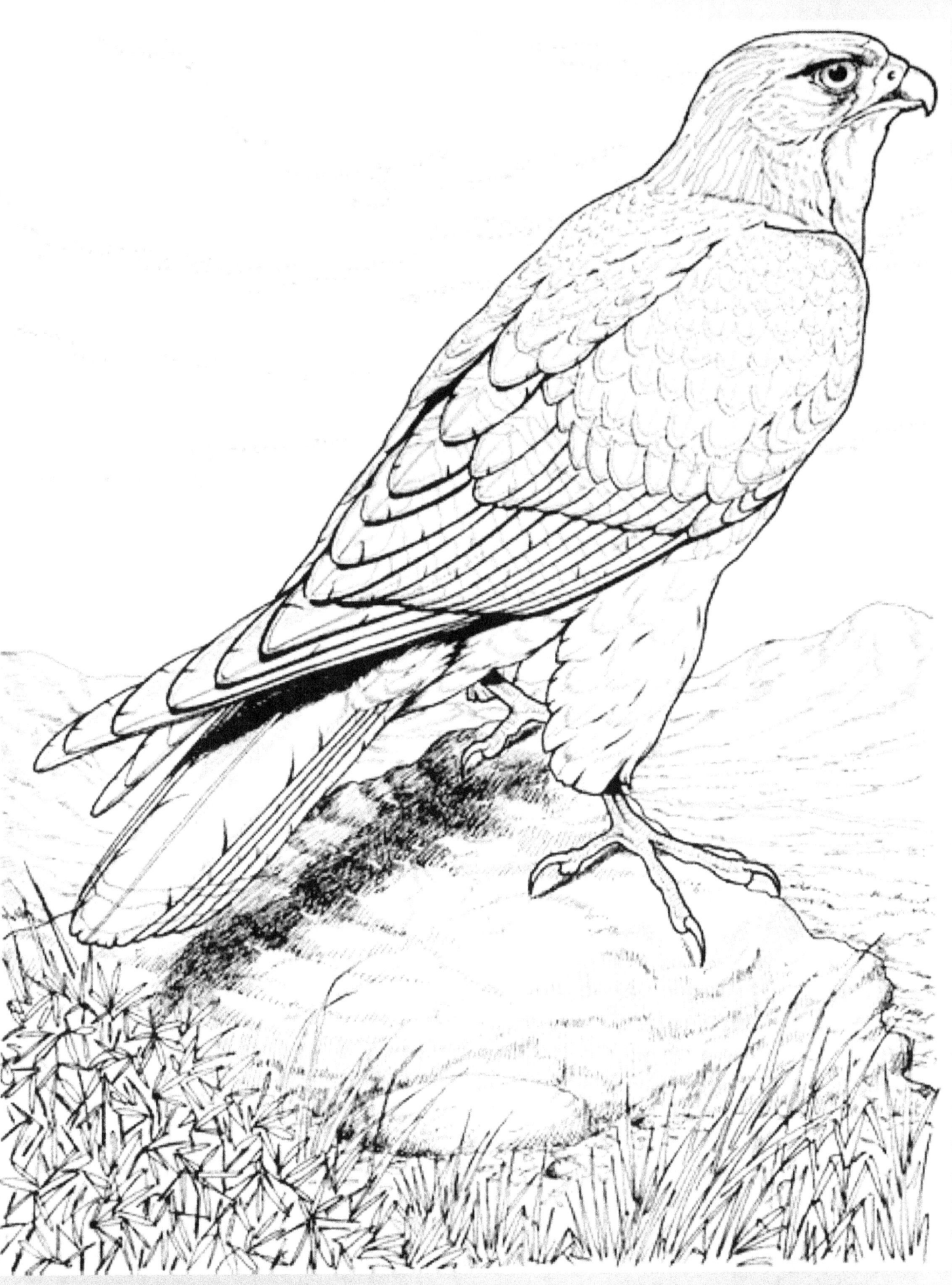

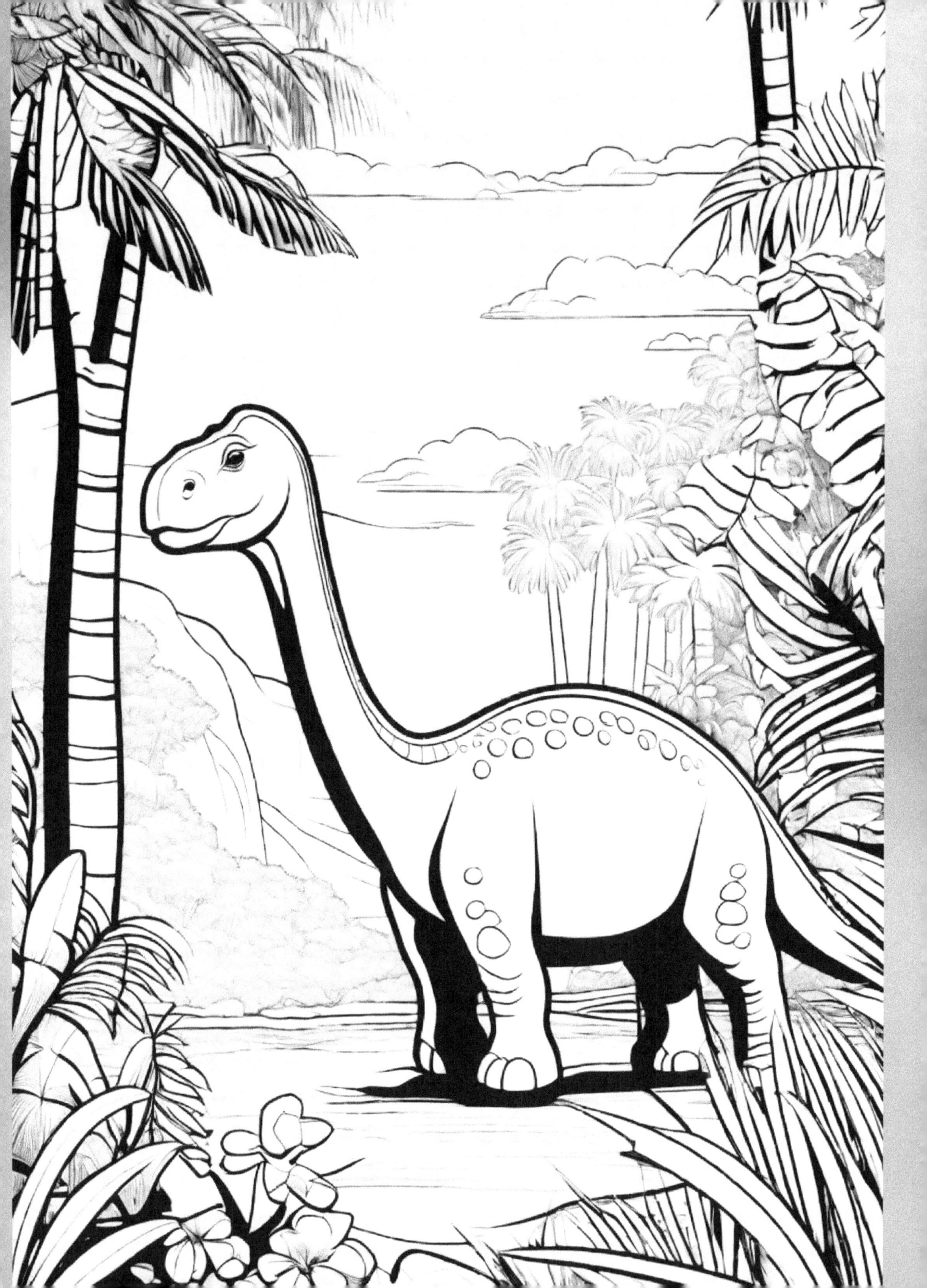

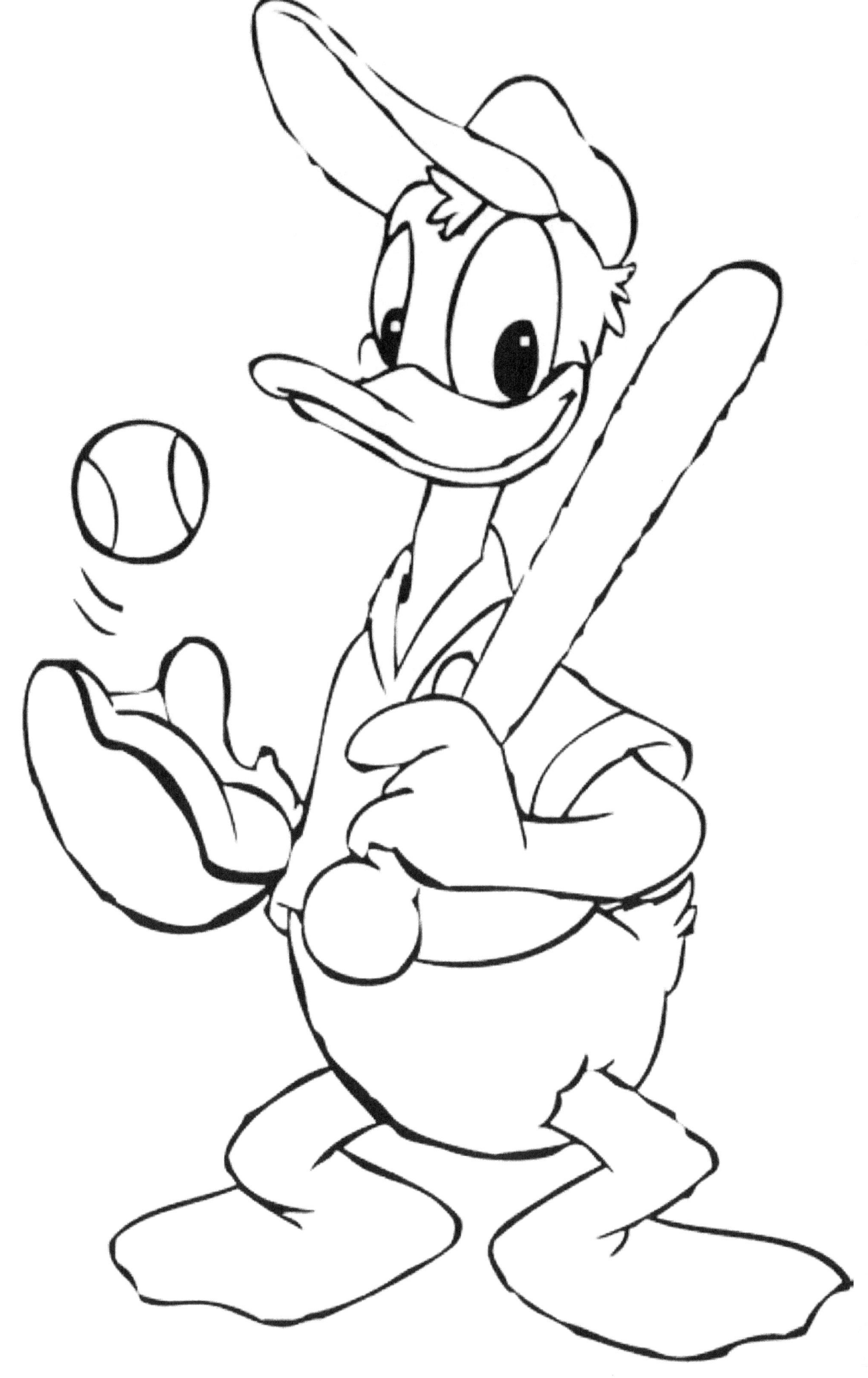

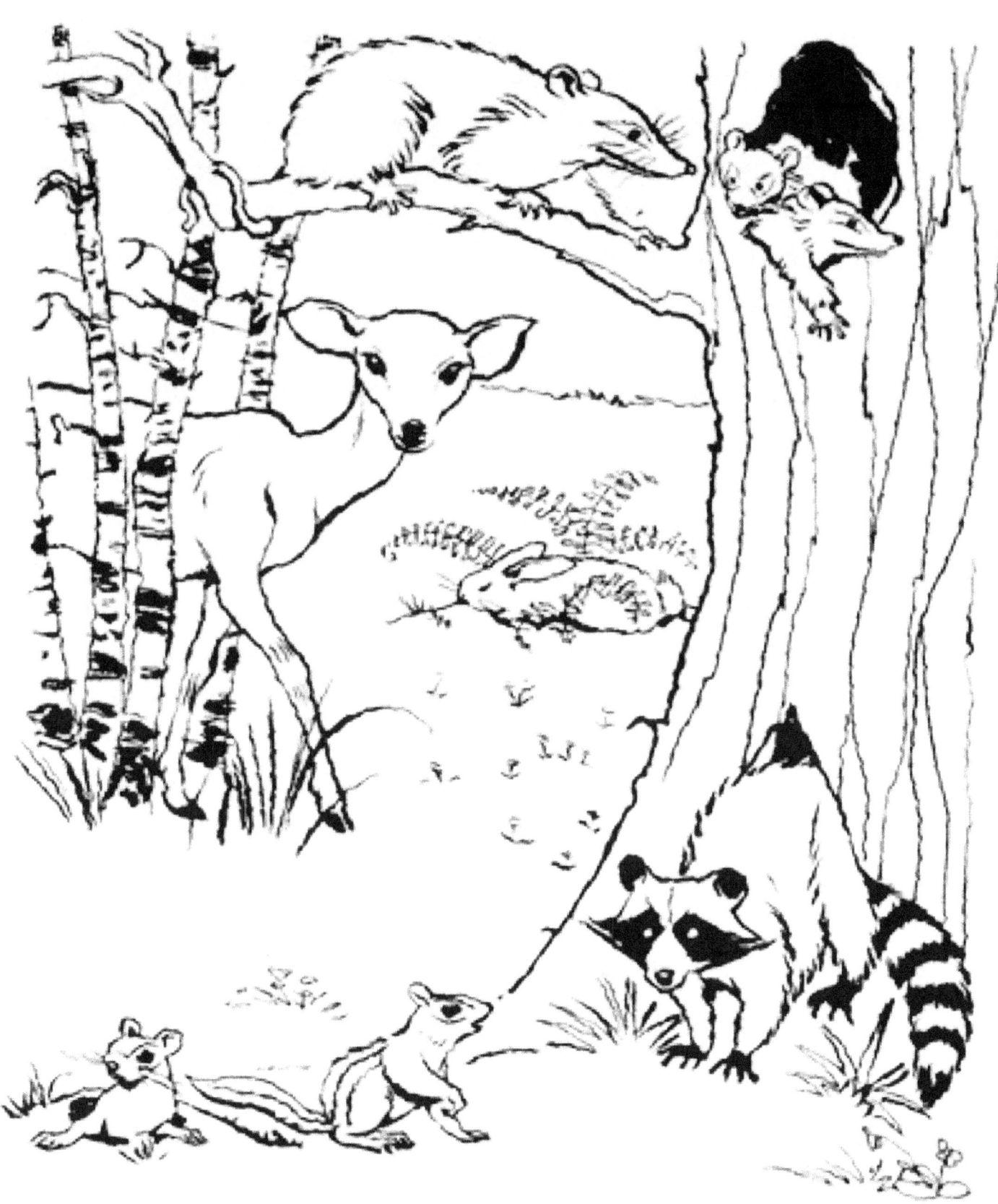

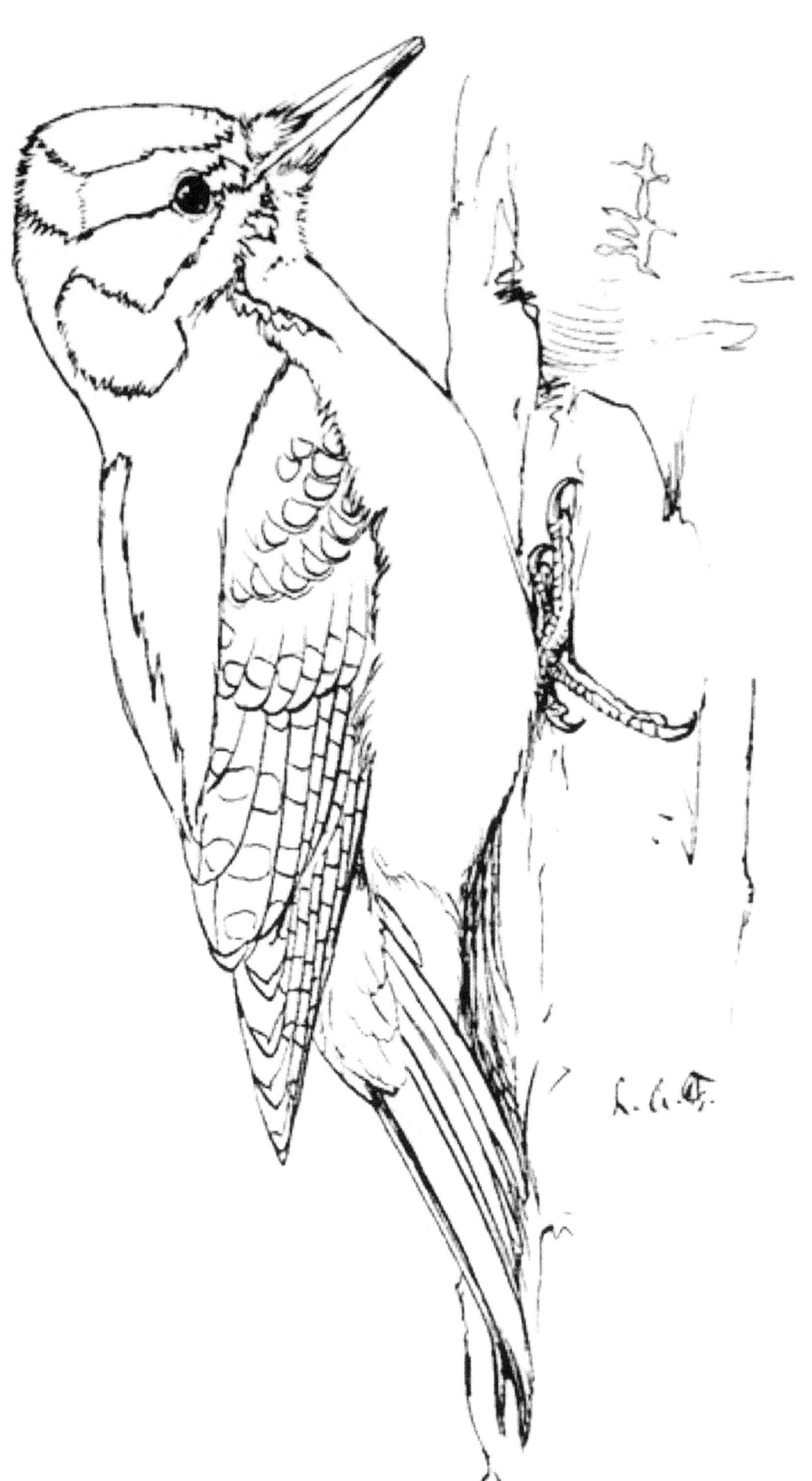

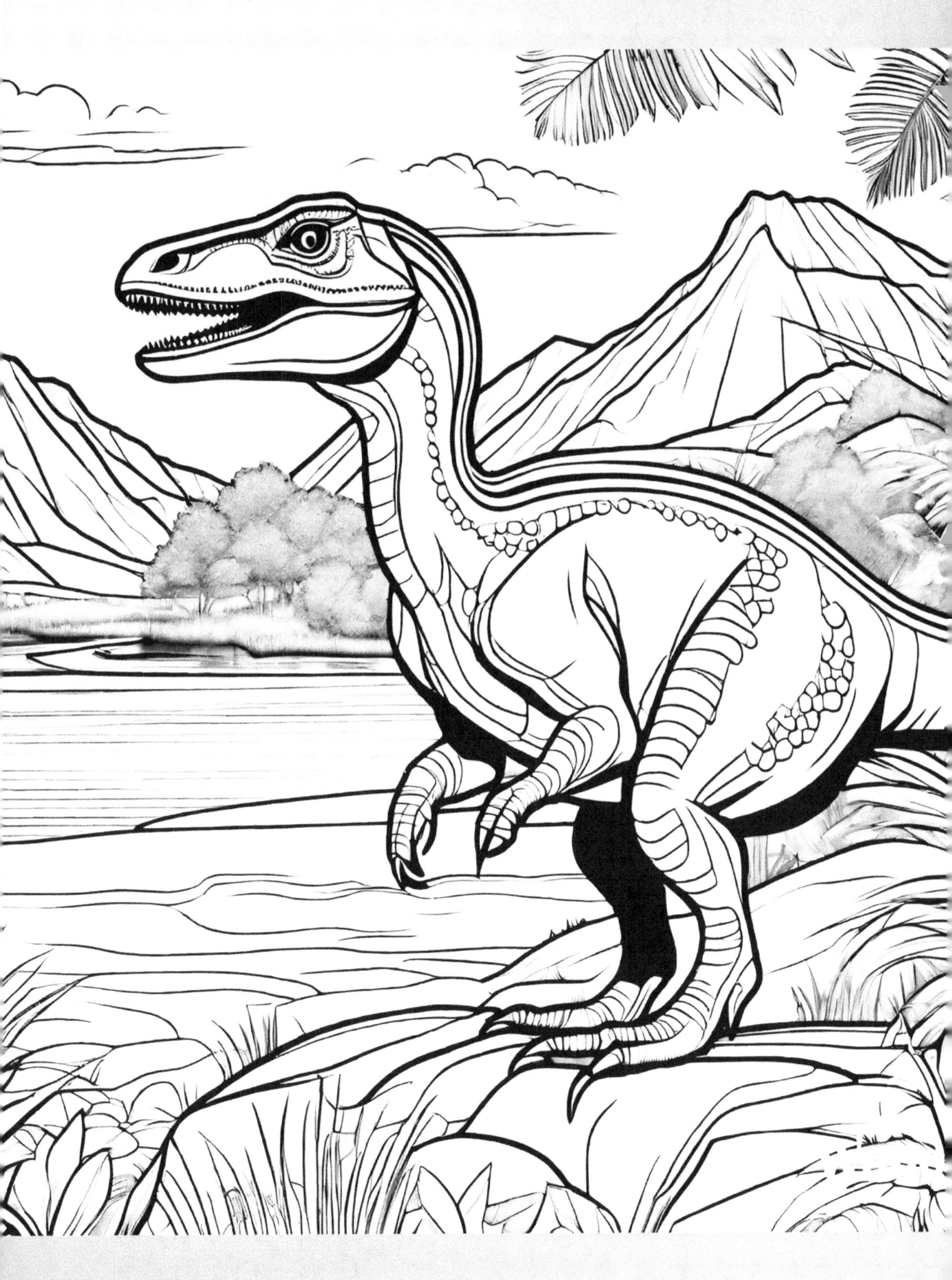

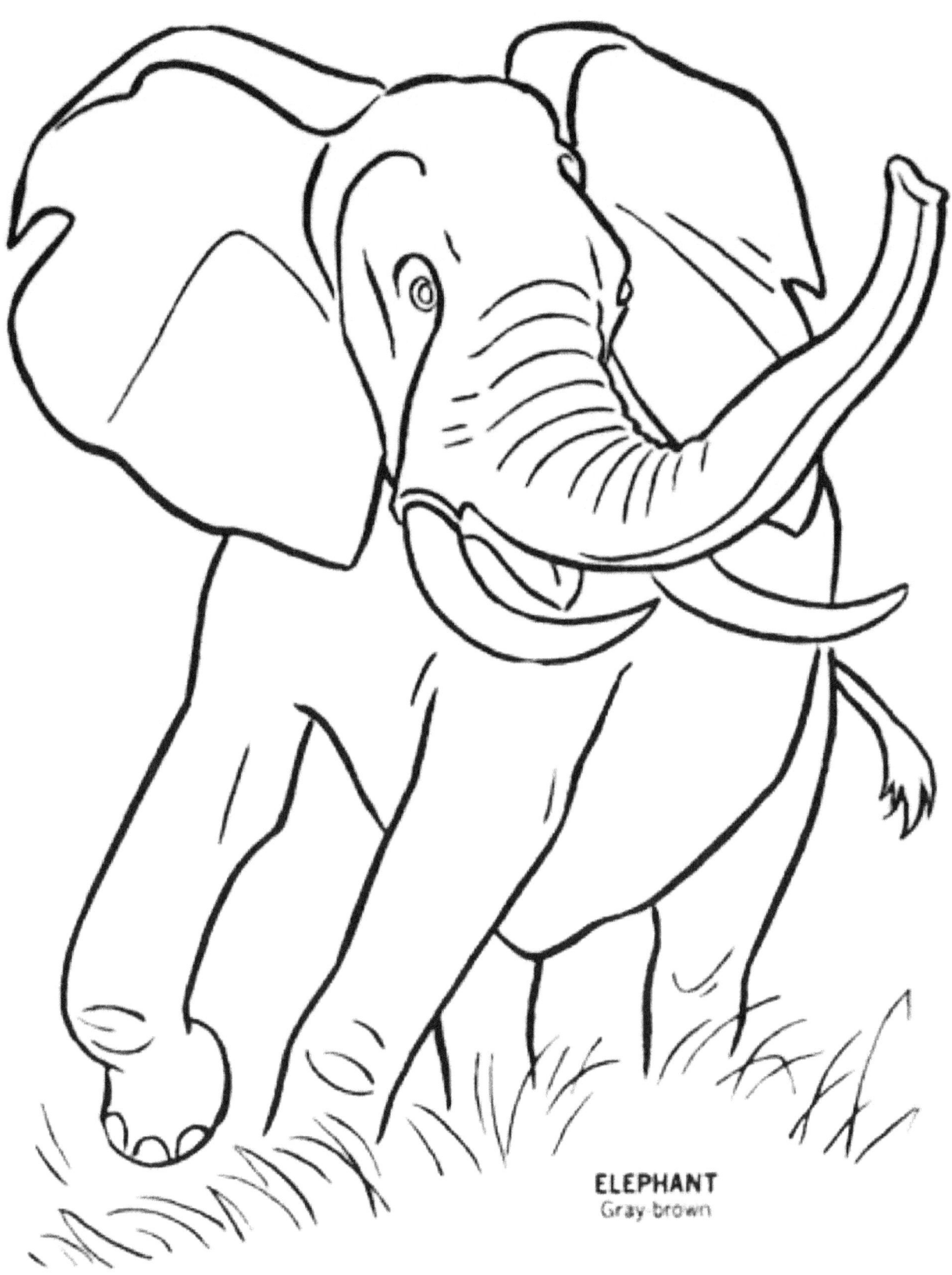

ELEPHANT
Gray-brown

African elephants are larger and wilder than those of India.
They may weigh from three to four tons.

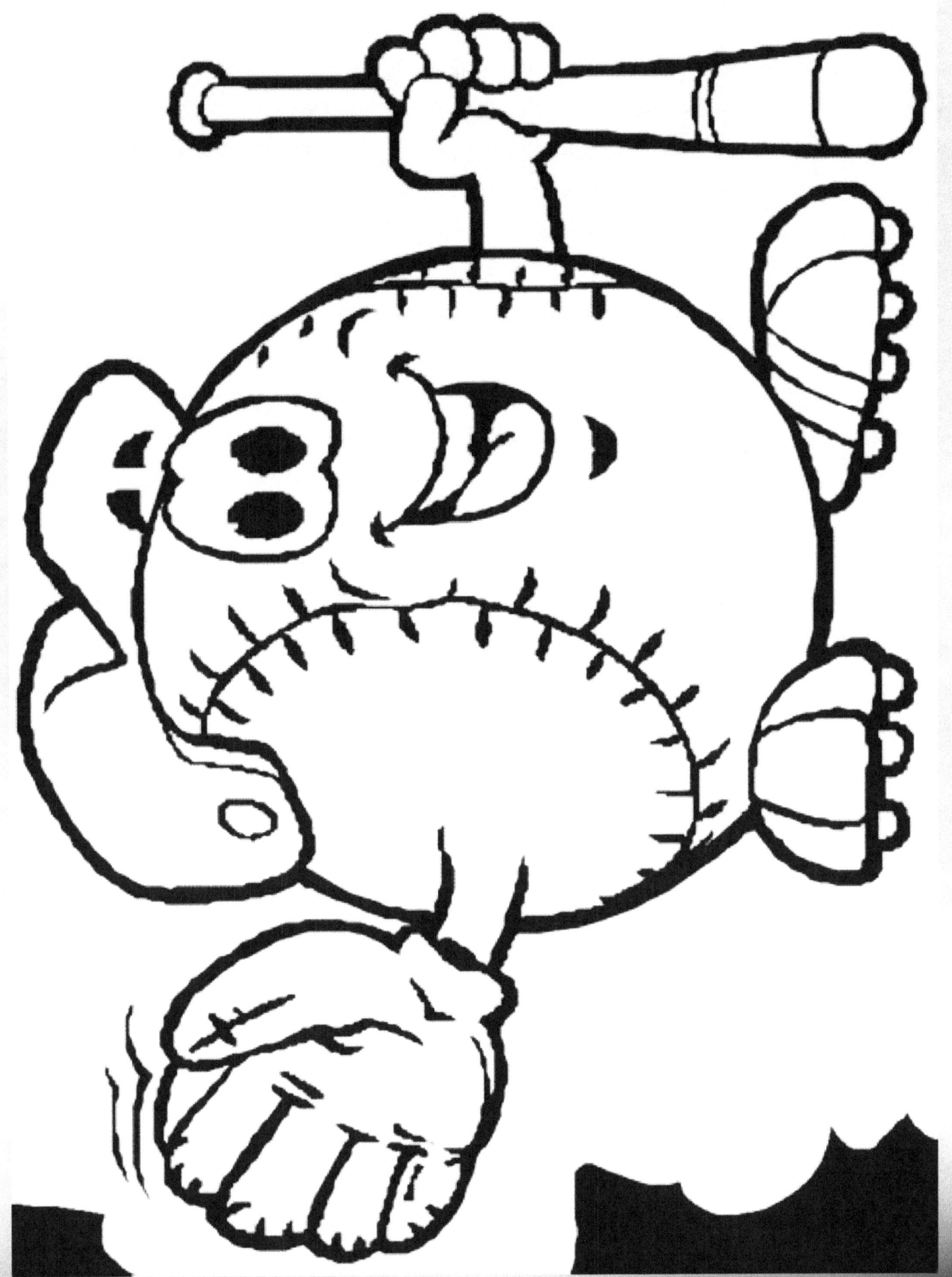

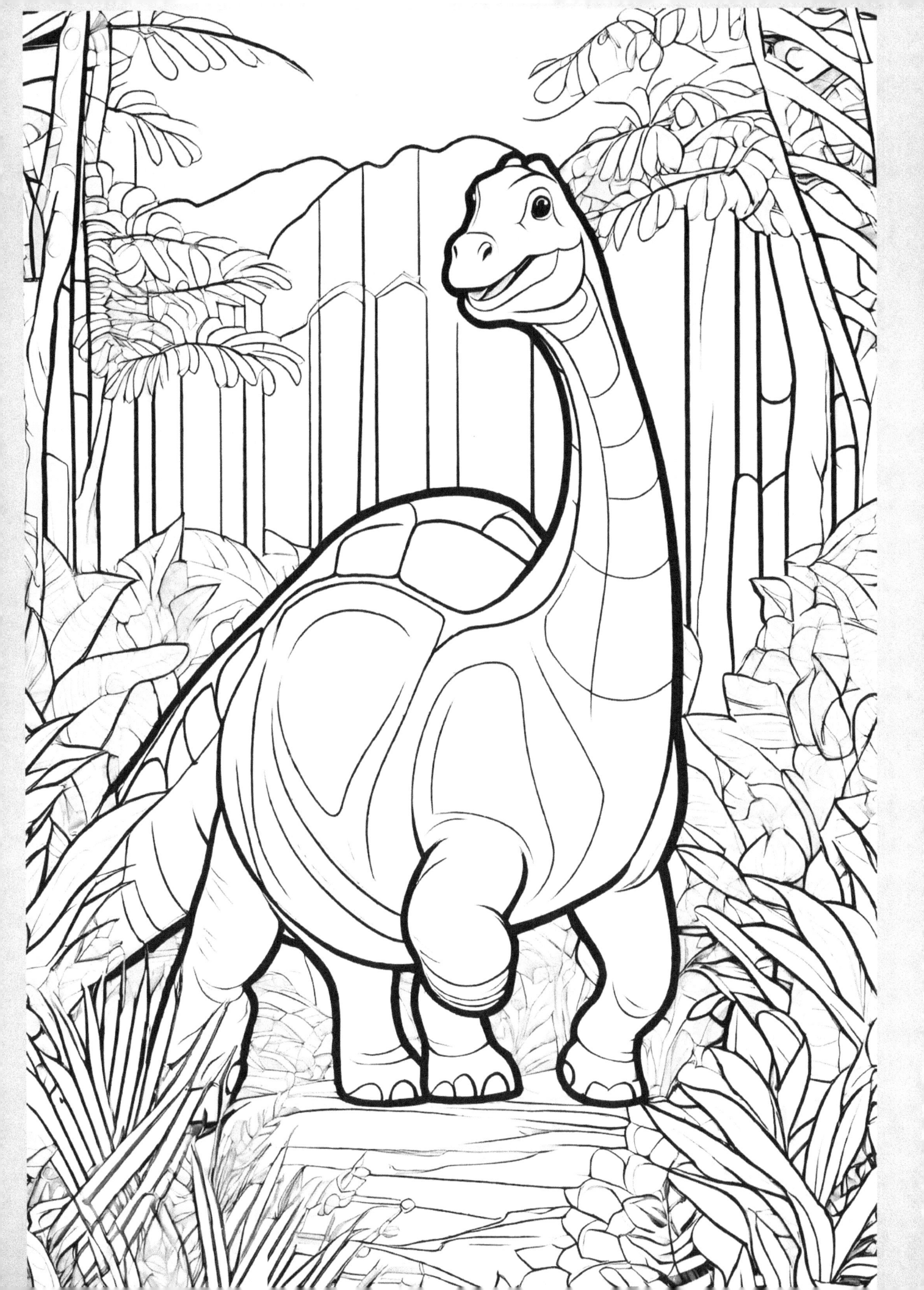

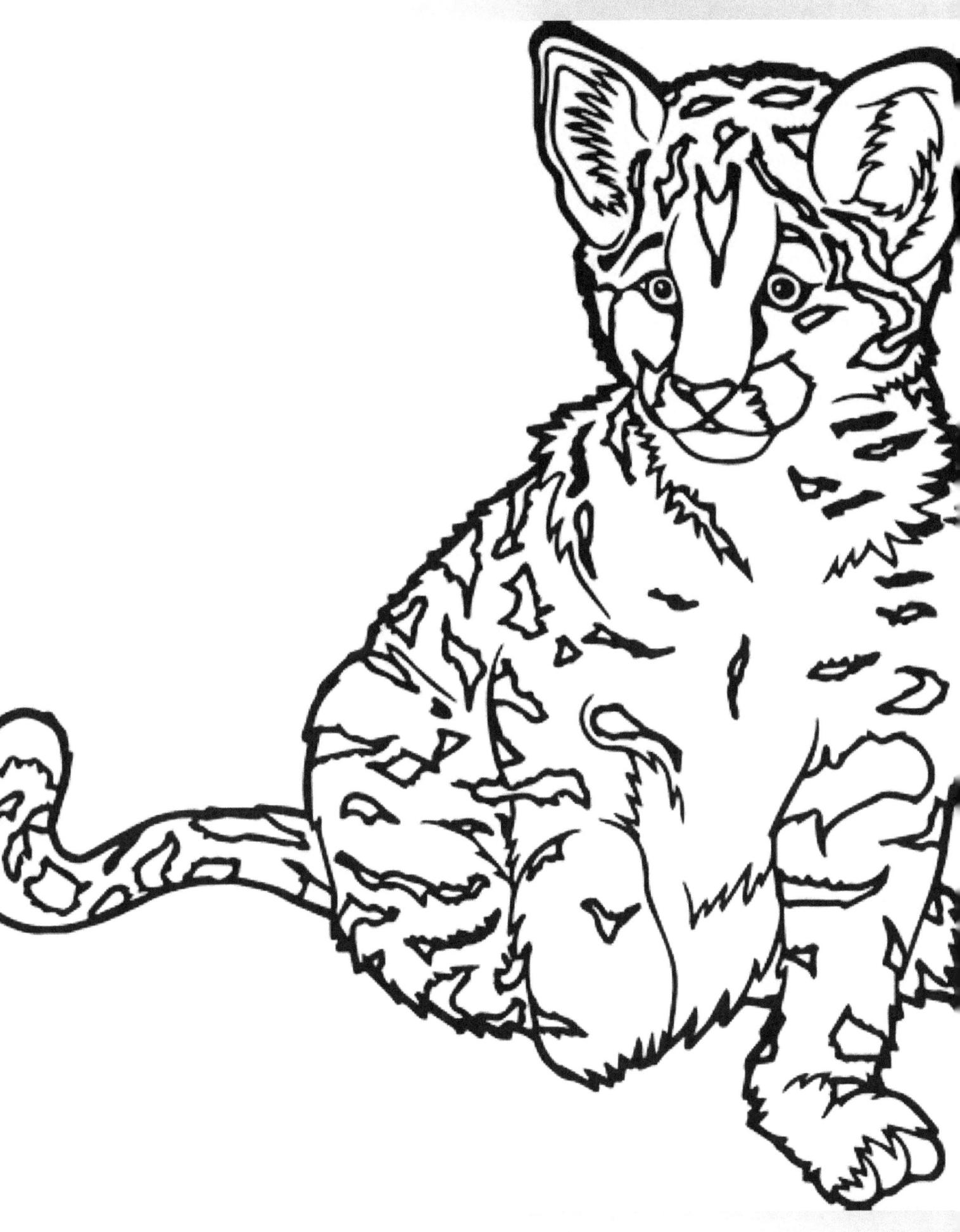

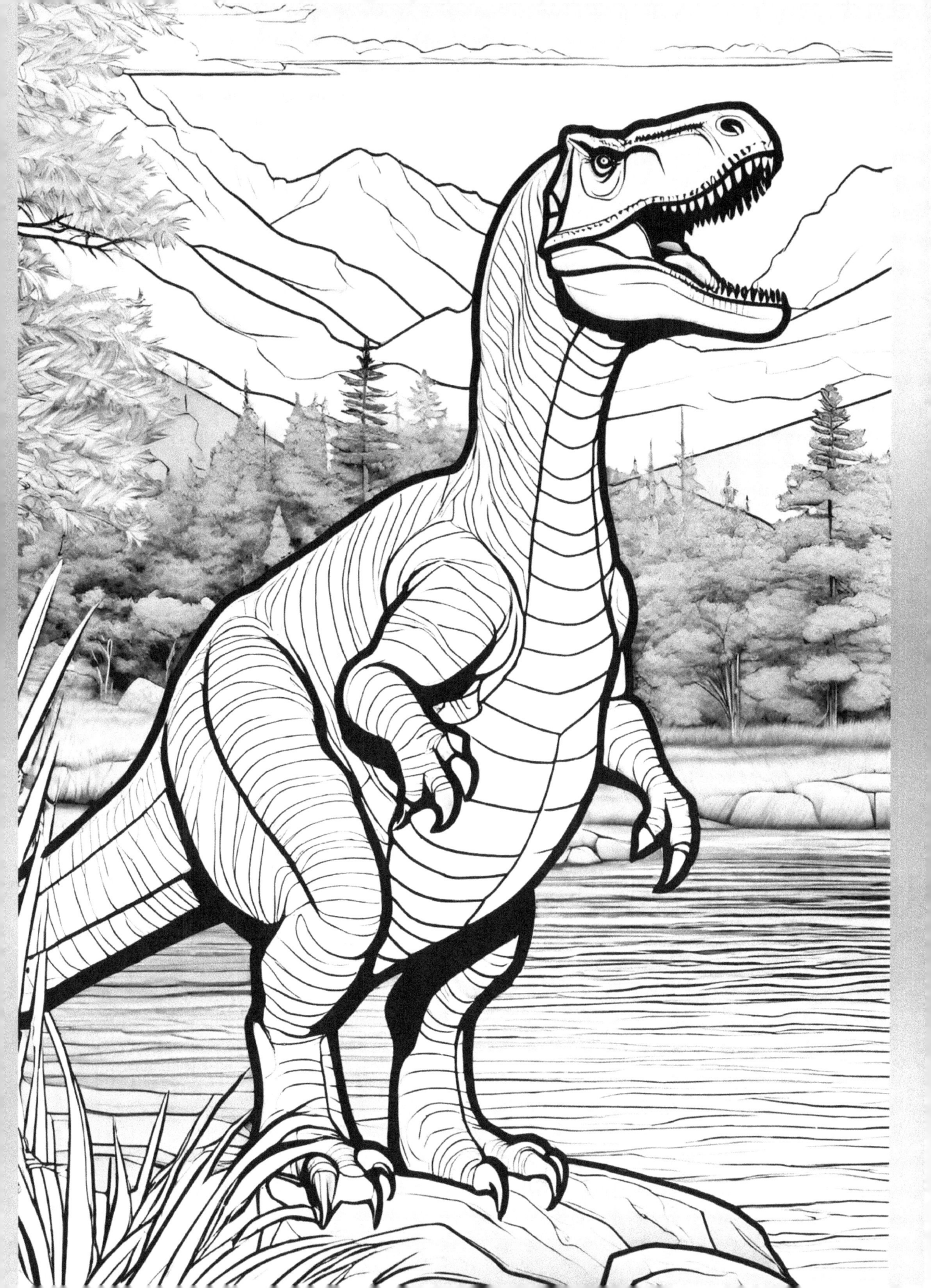

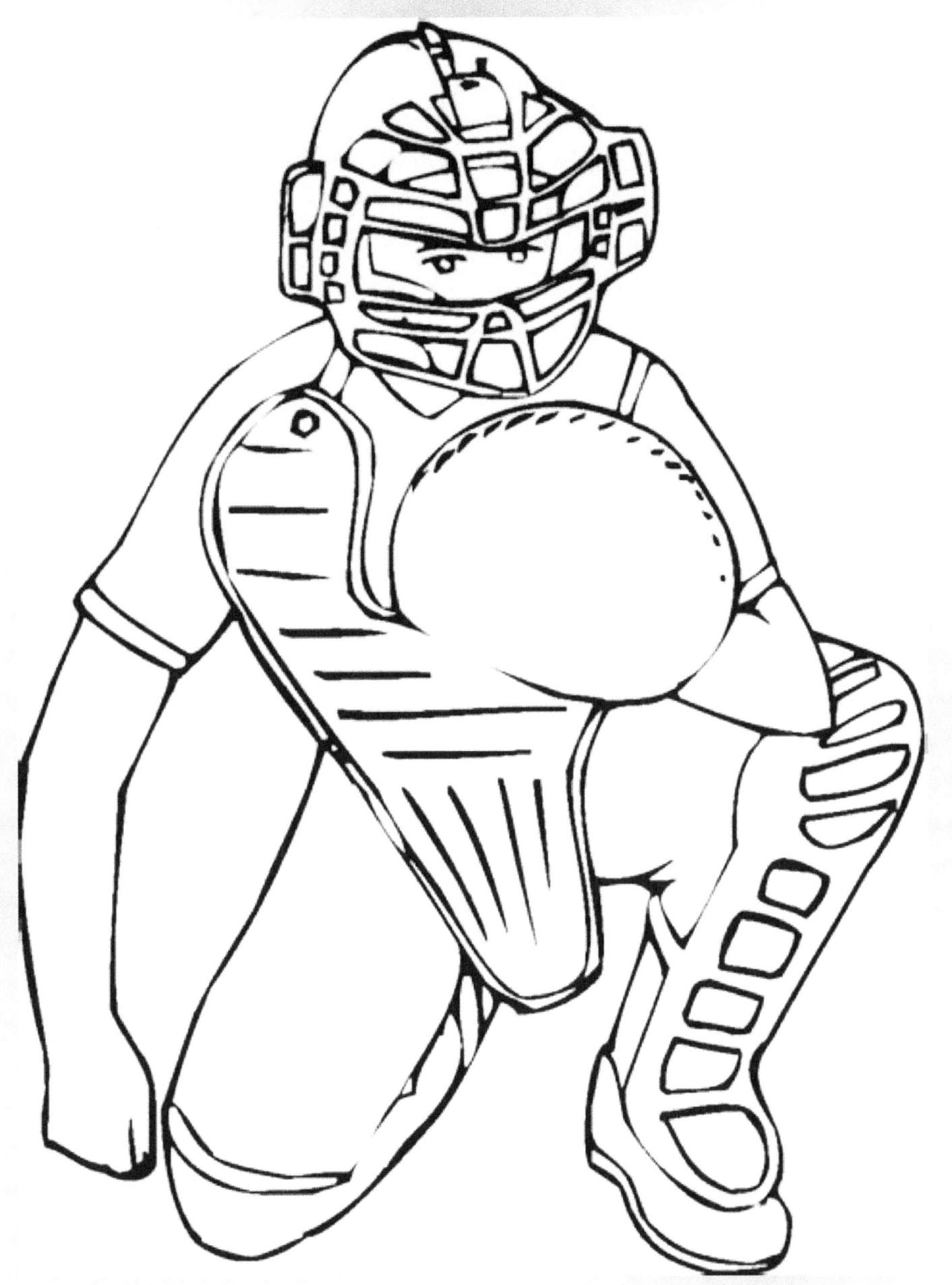

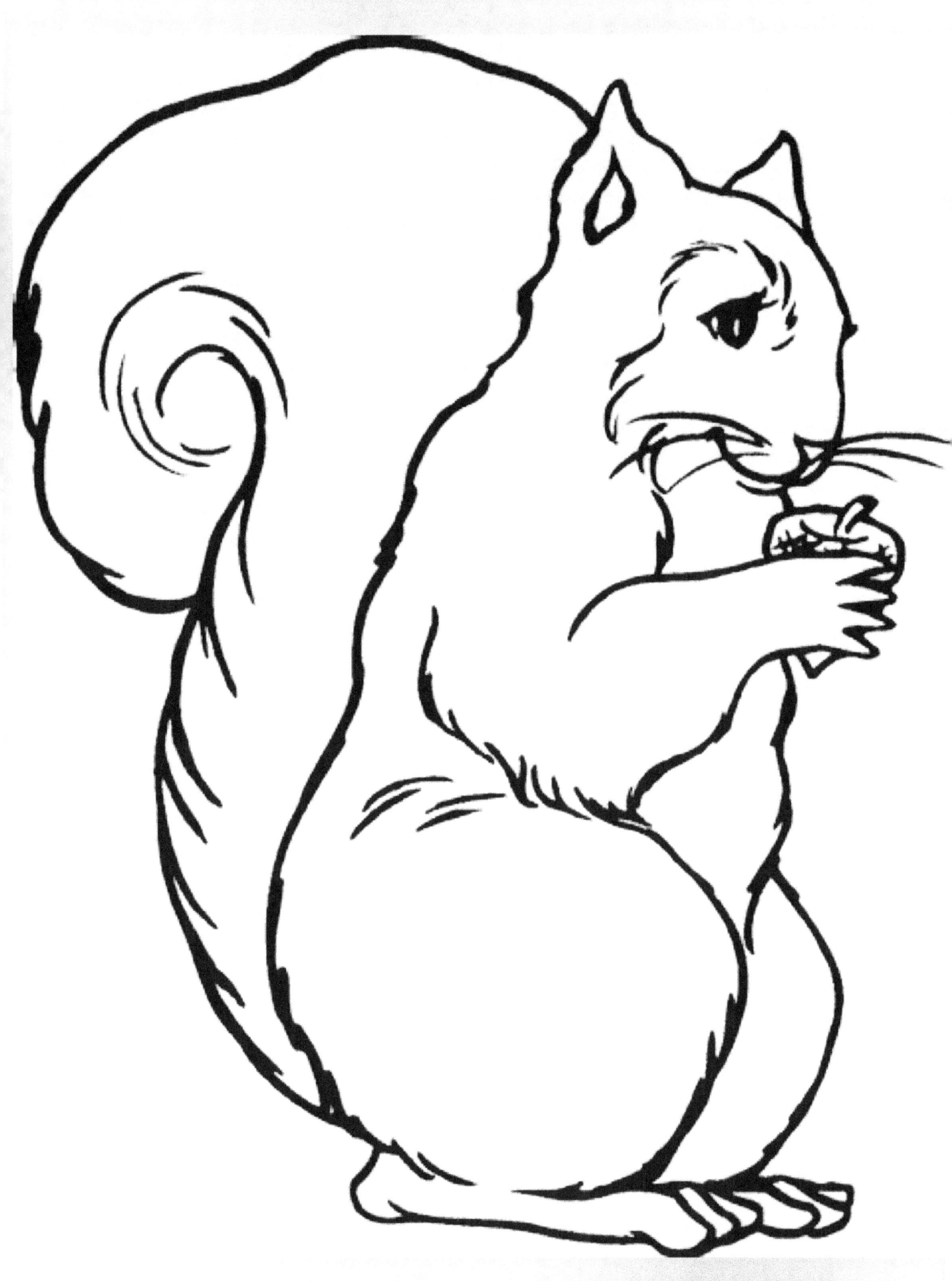

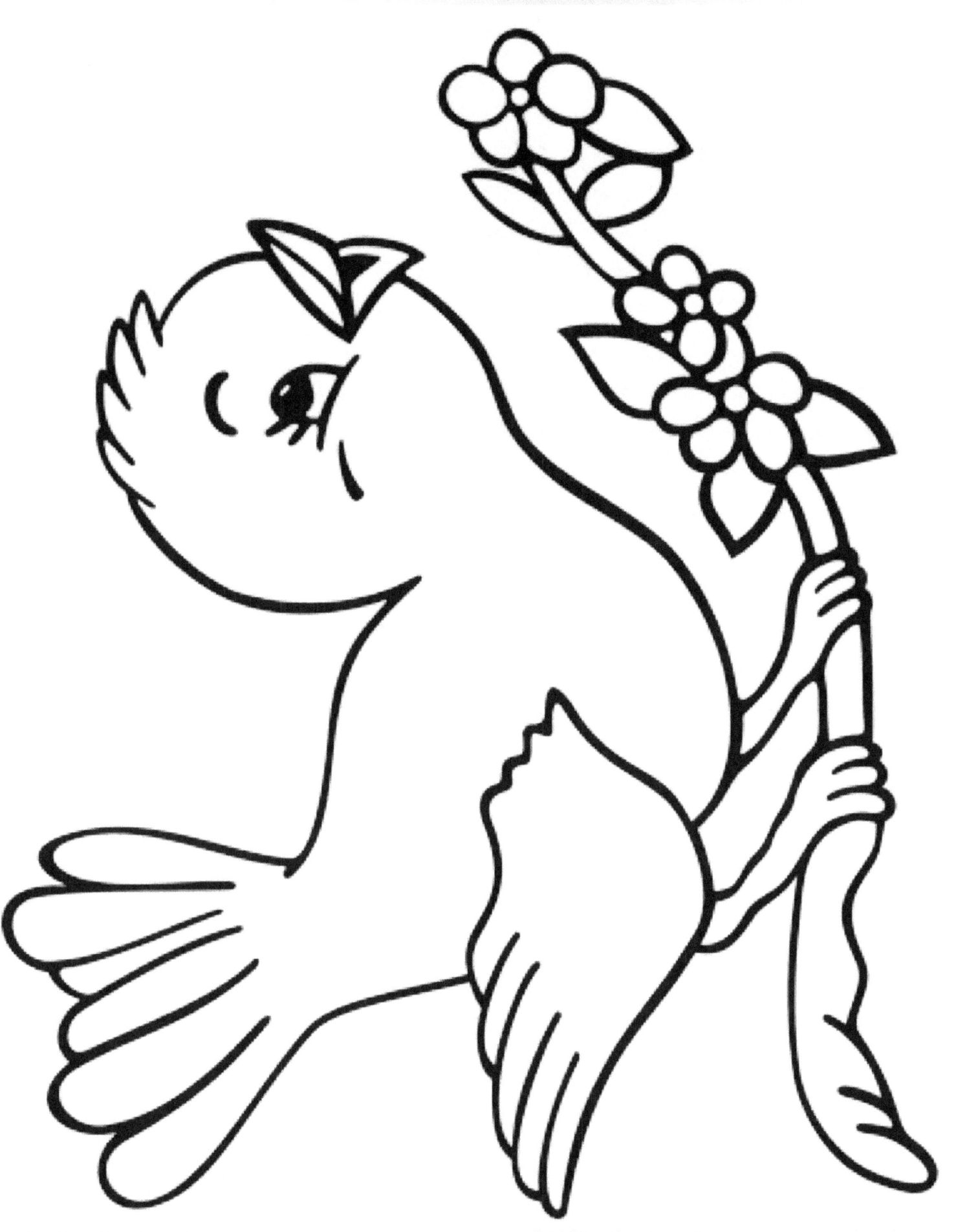

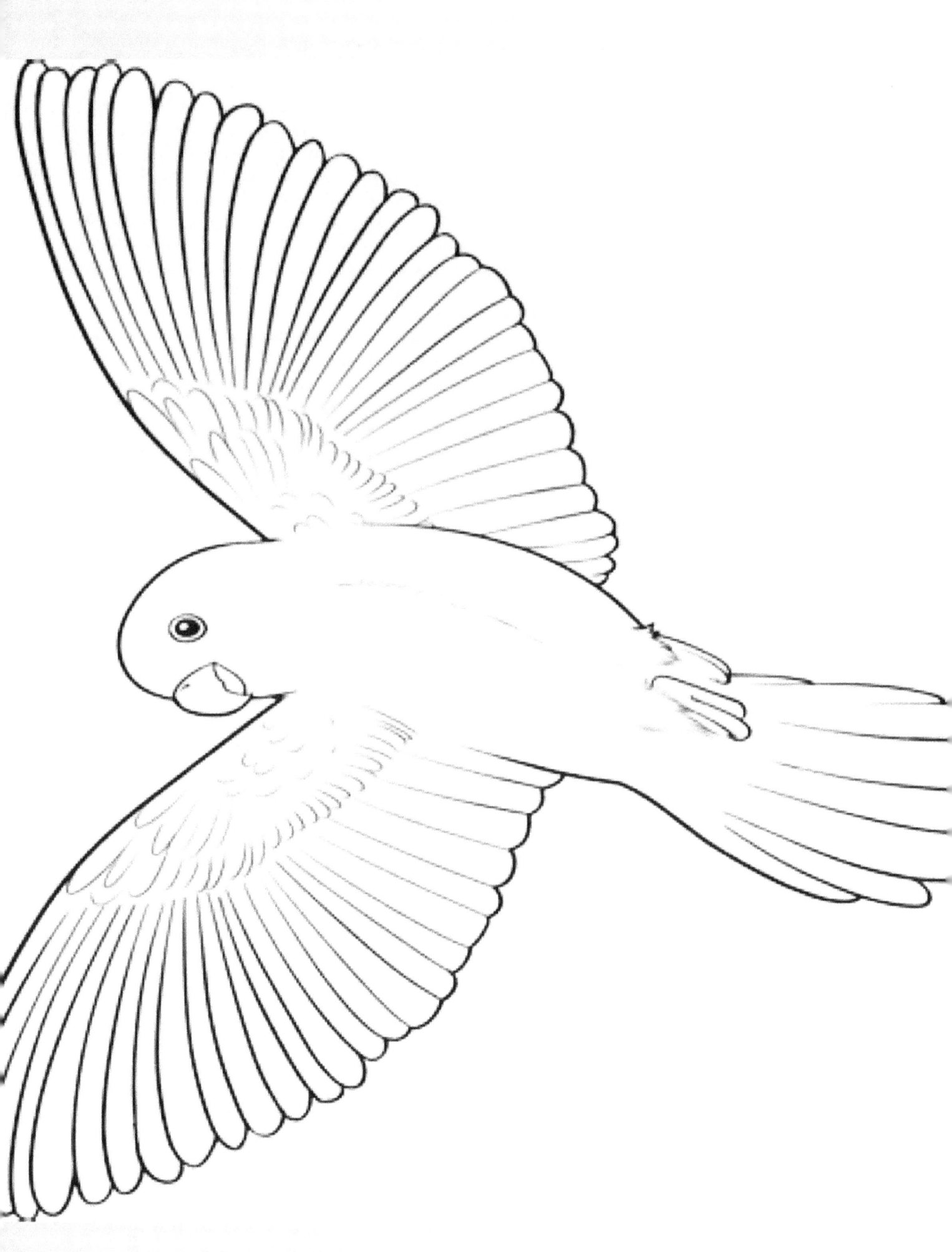

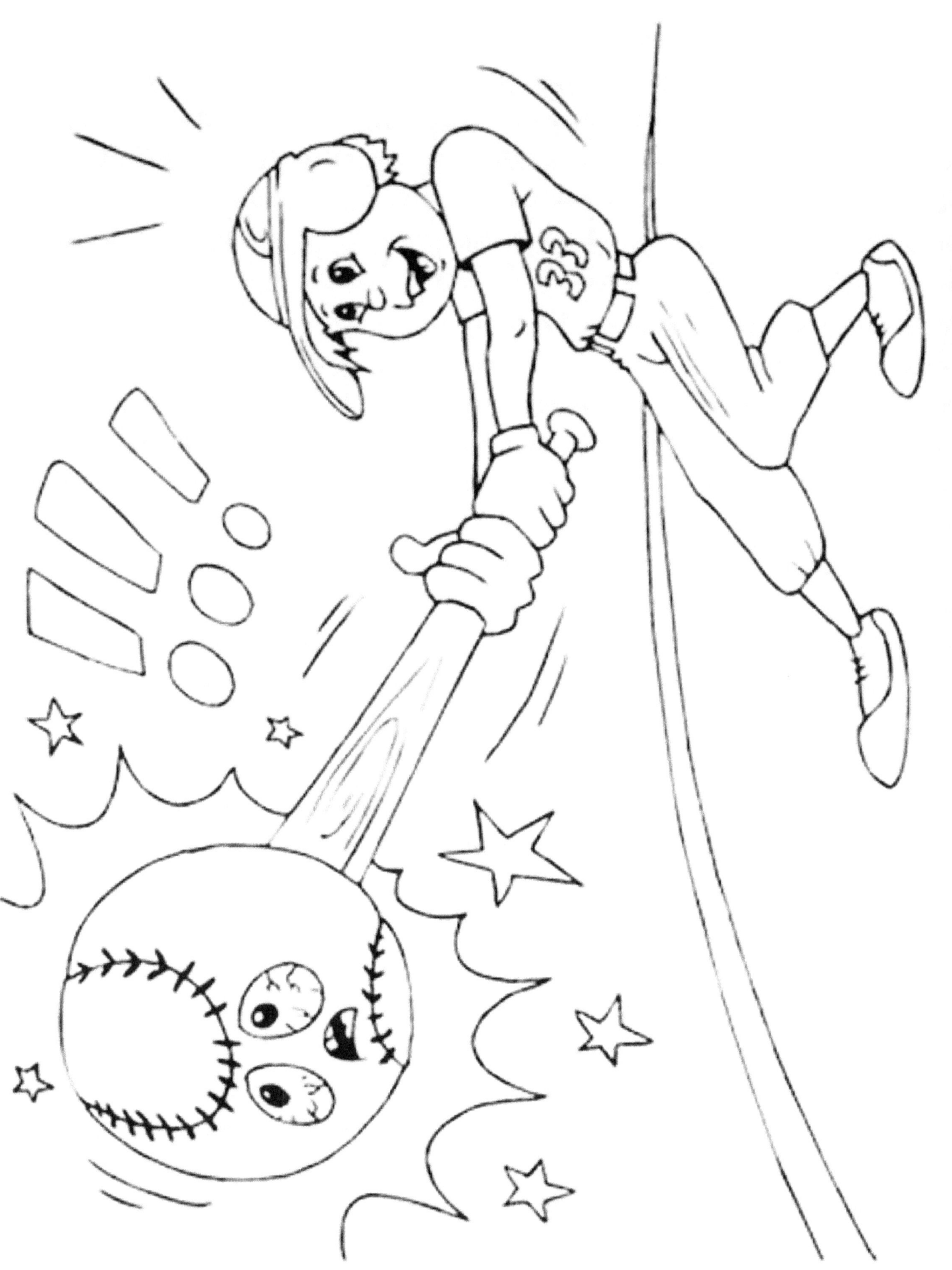

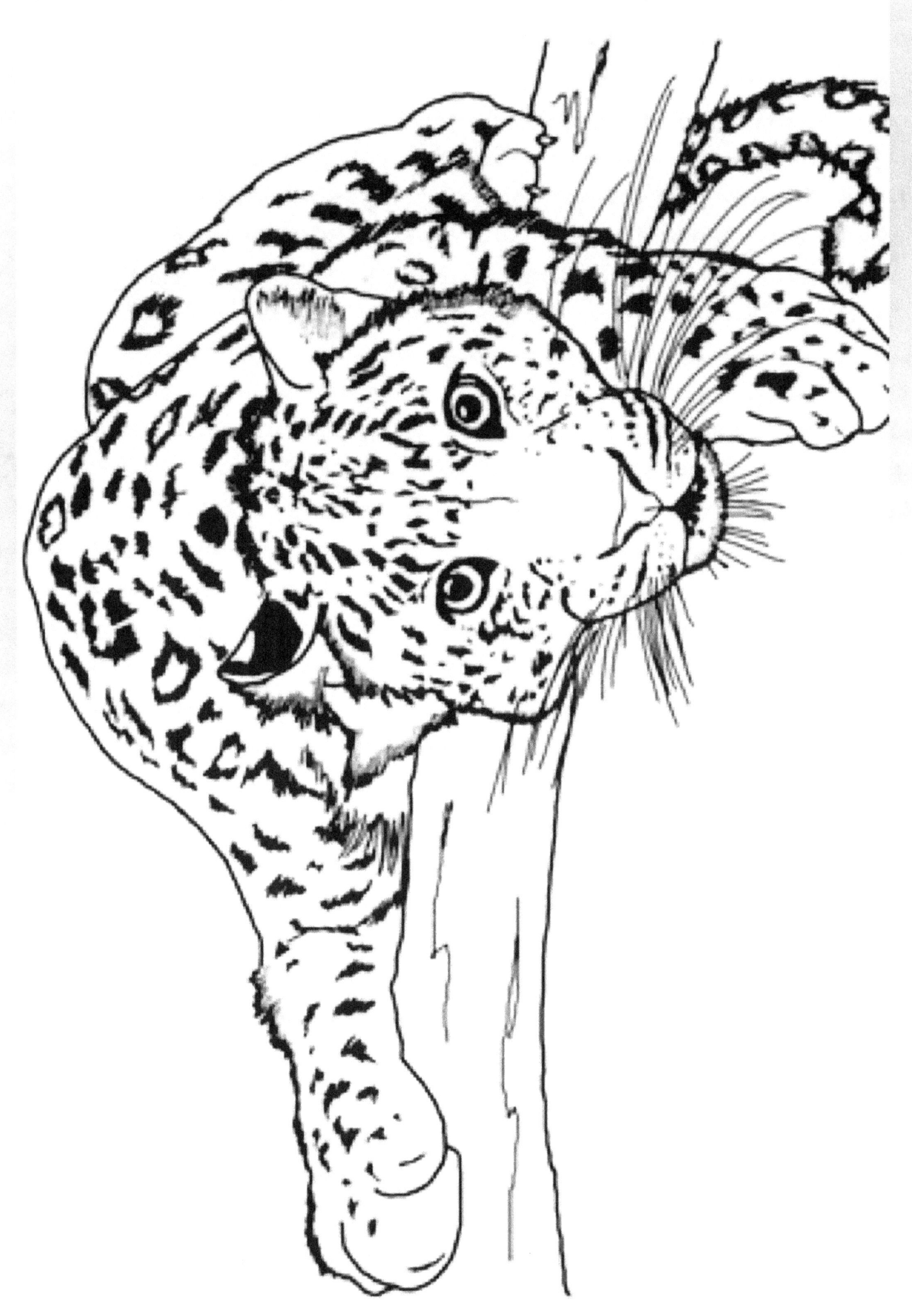

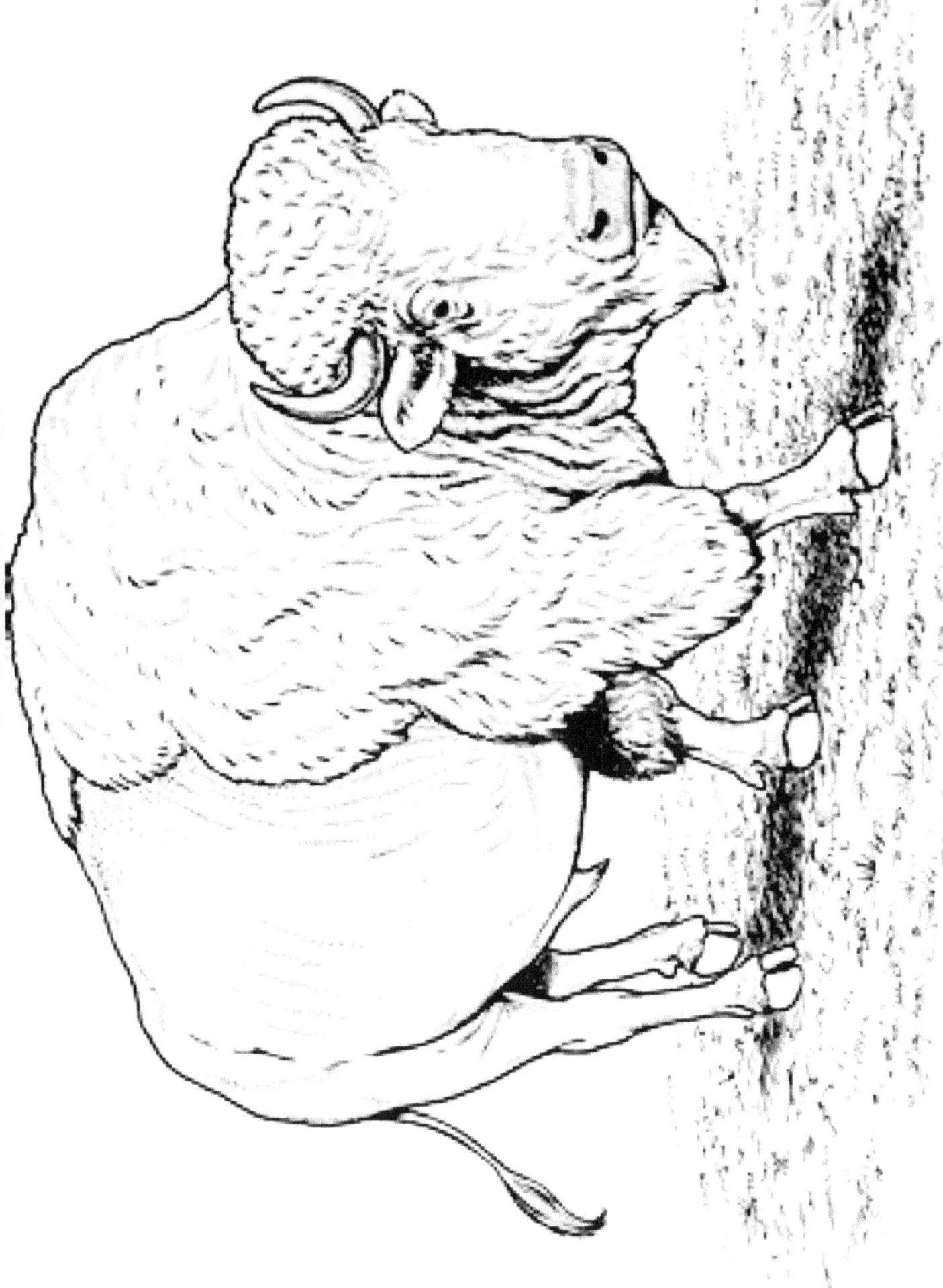

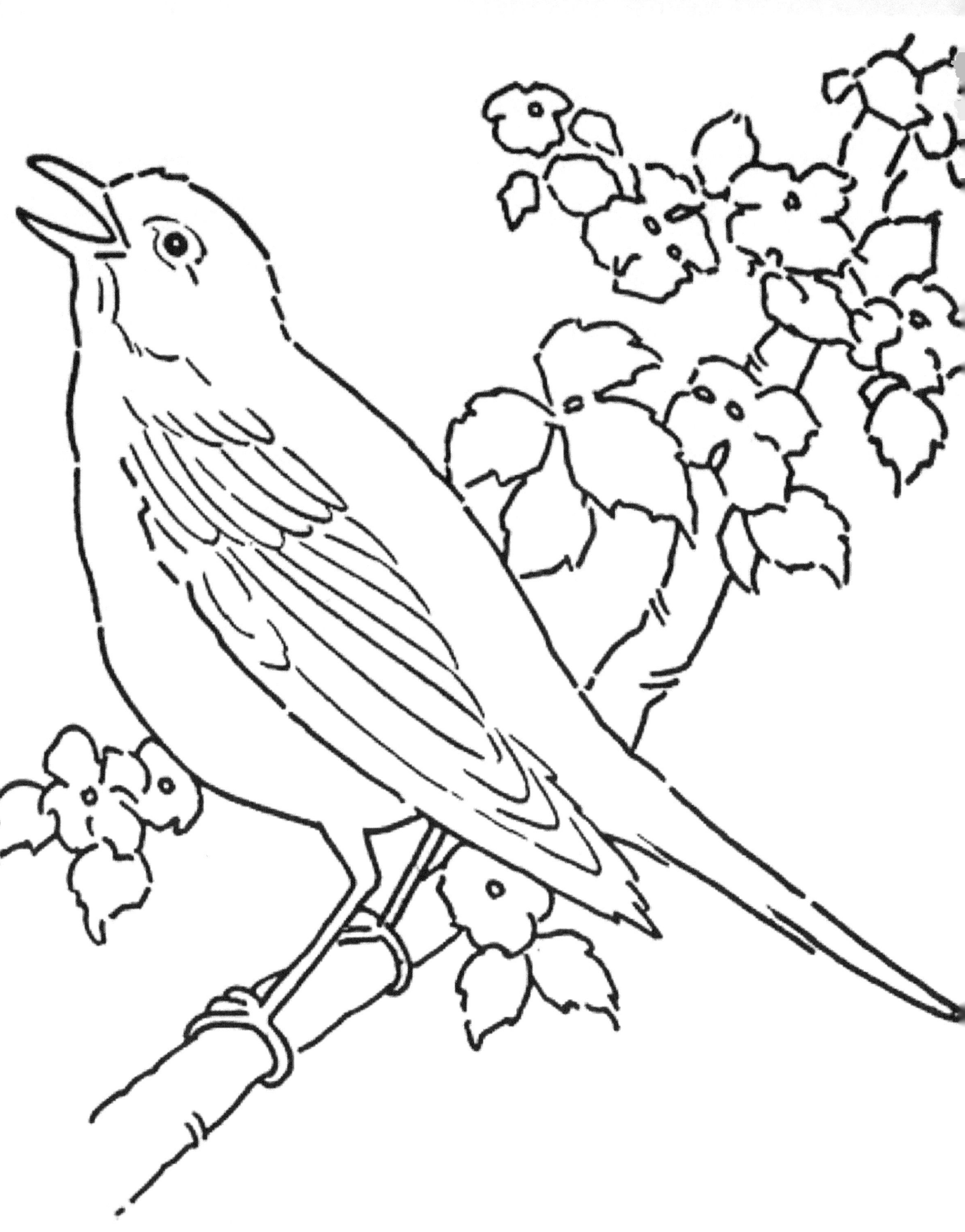

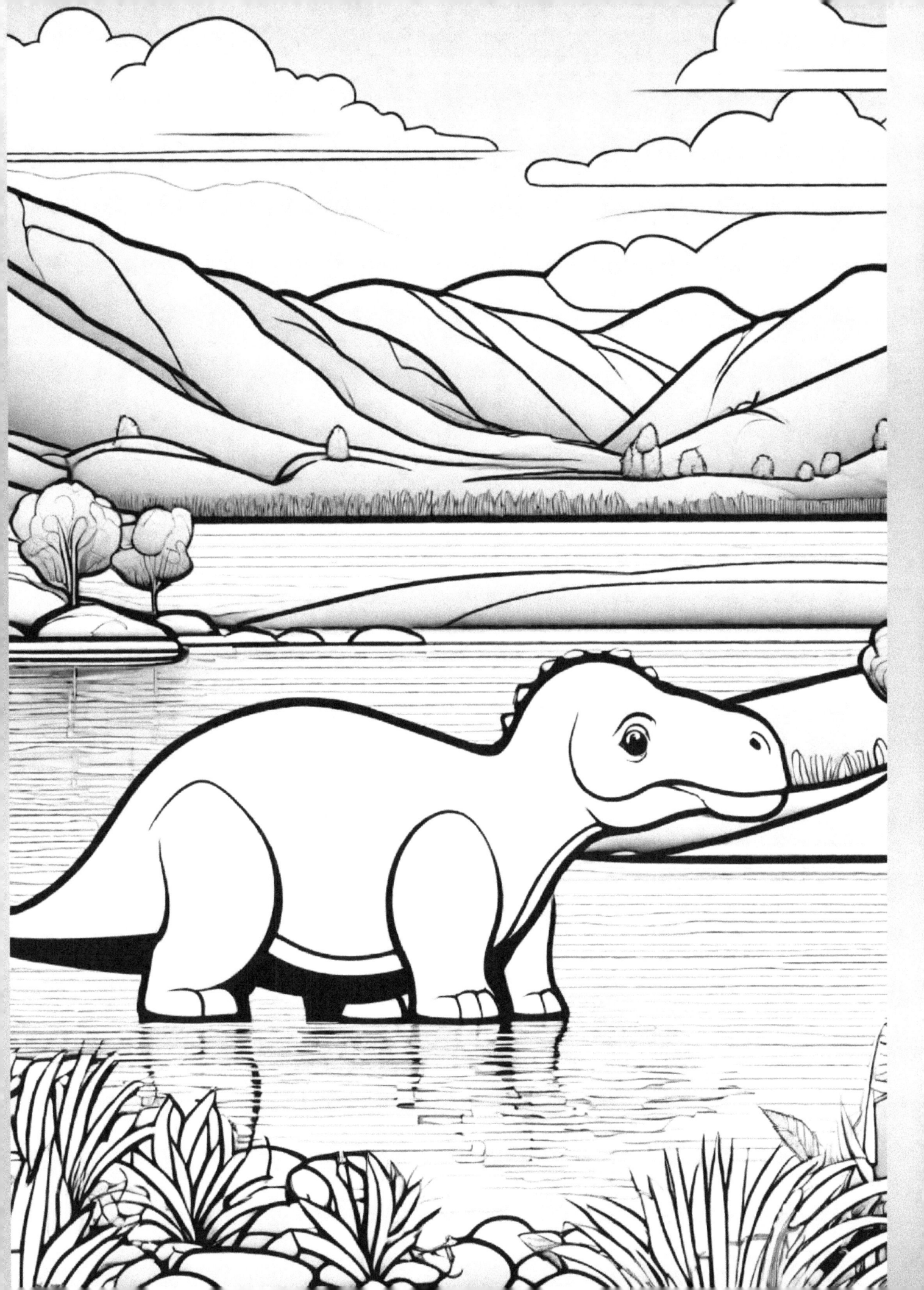

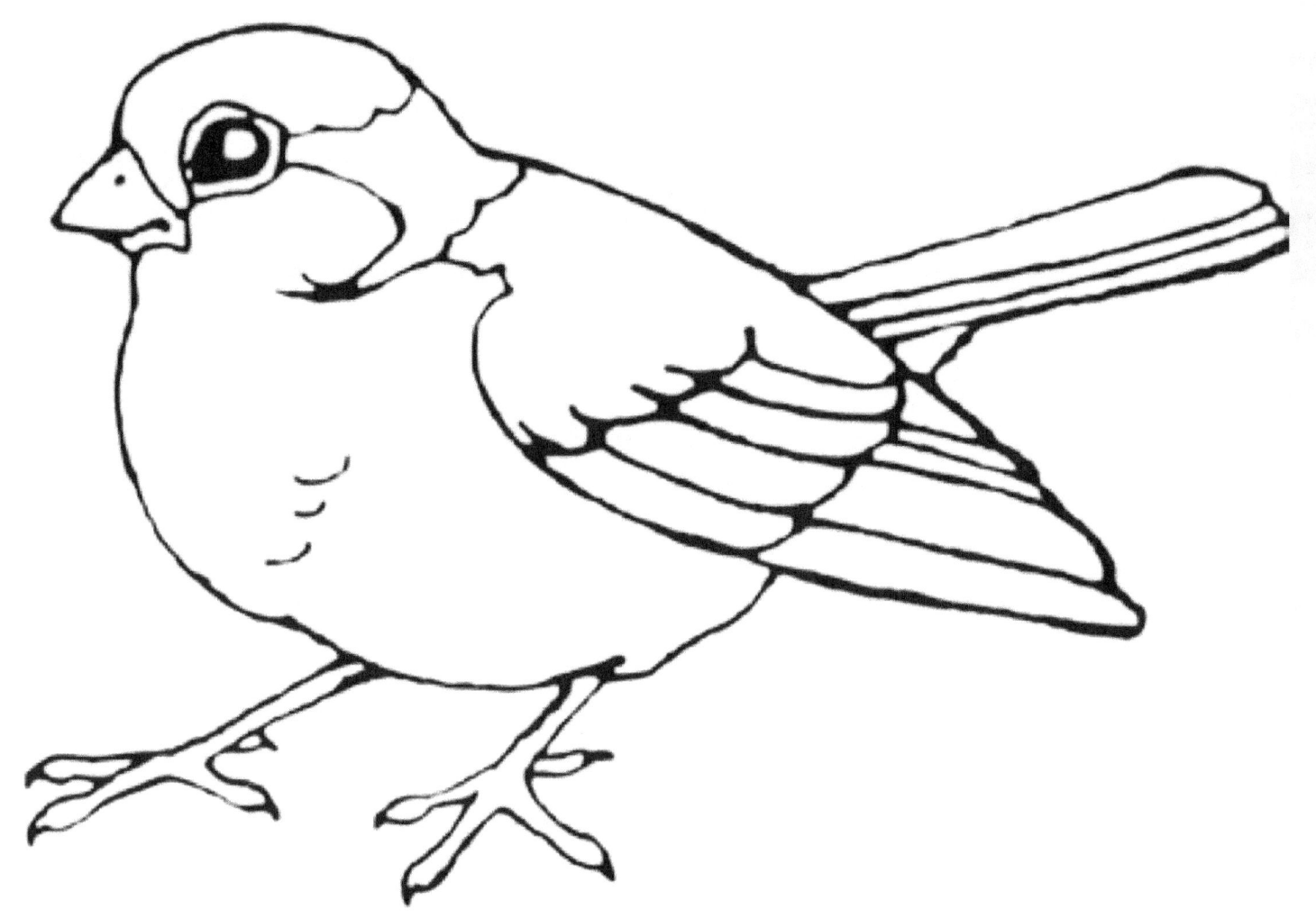

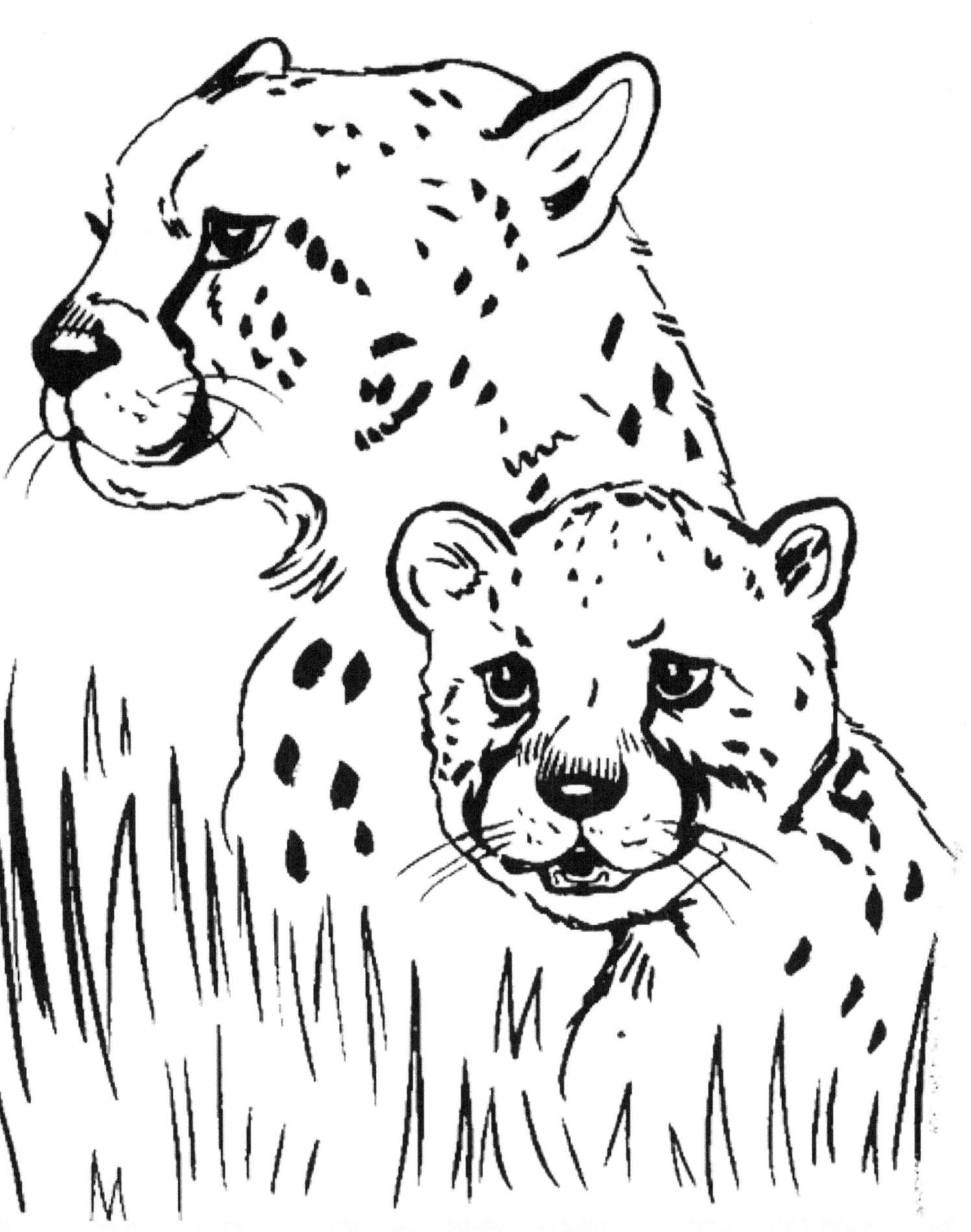

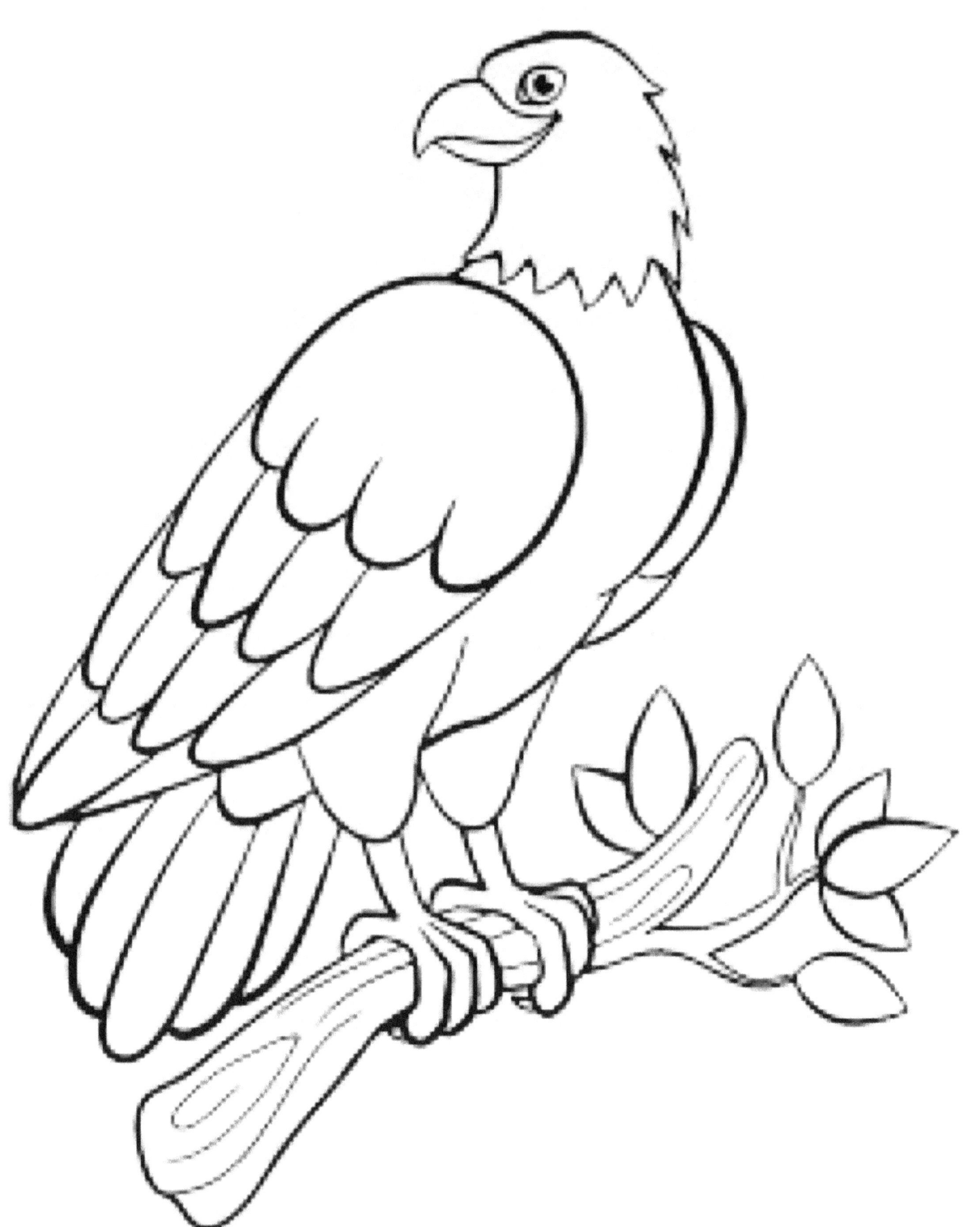

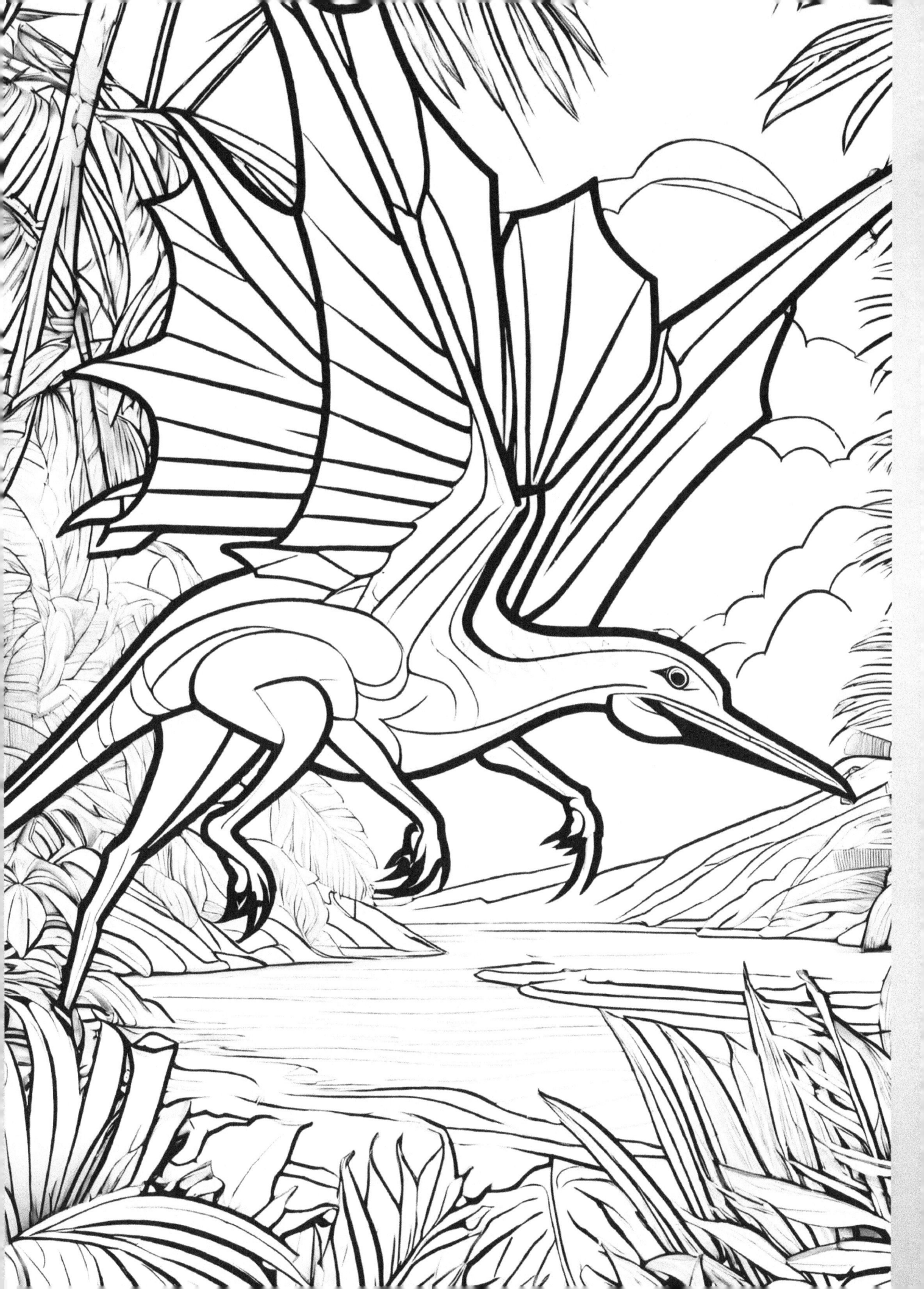

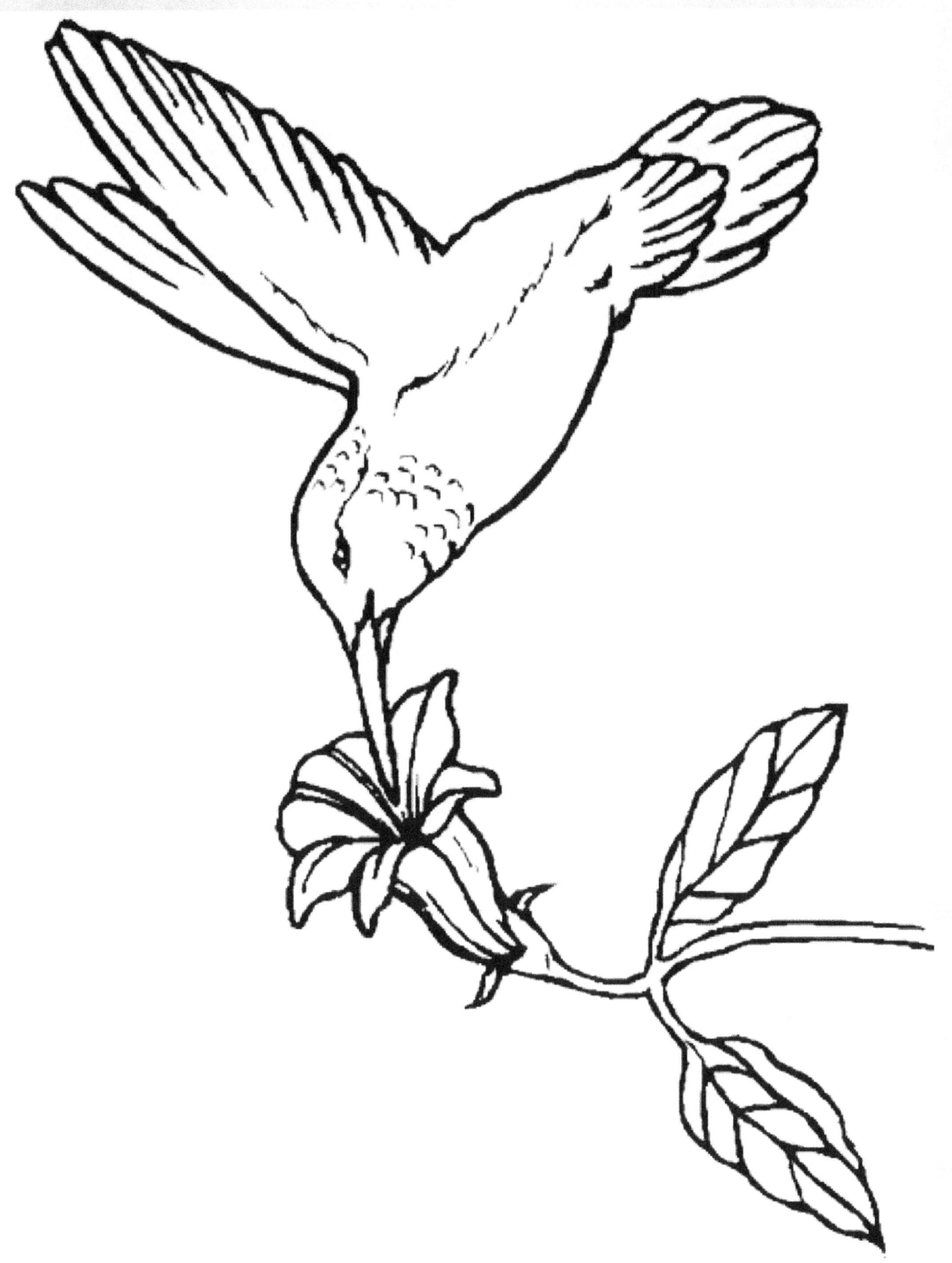

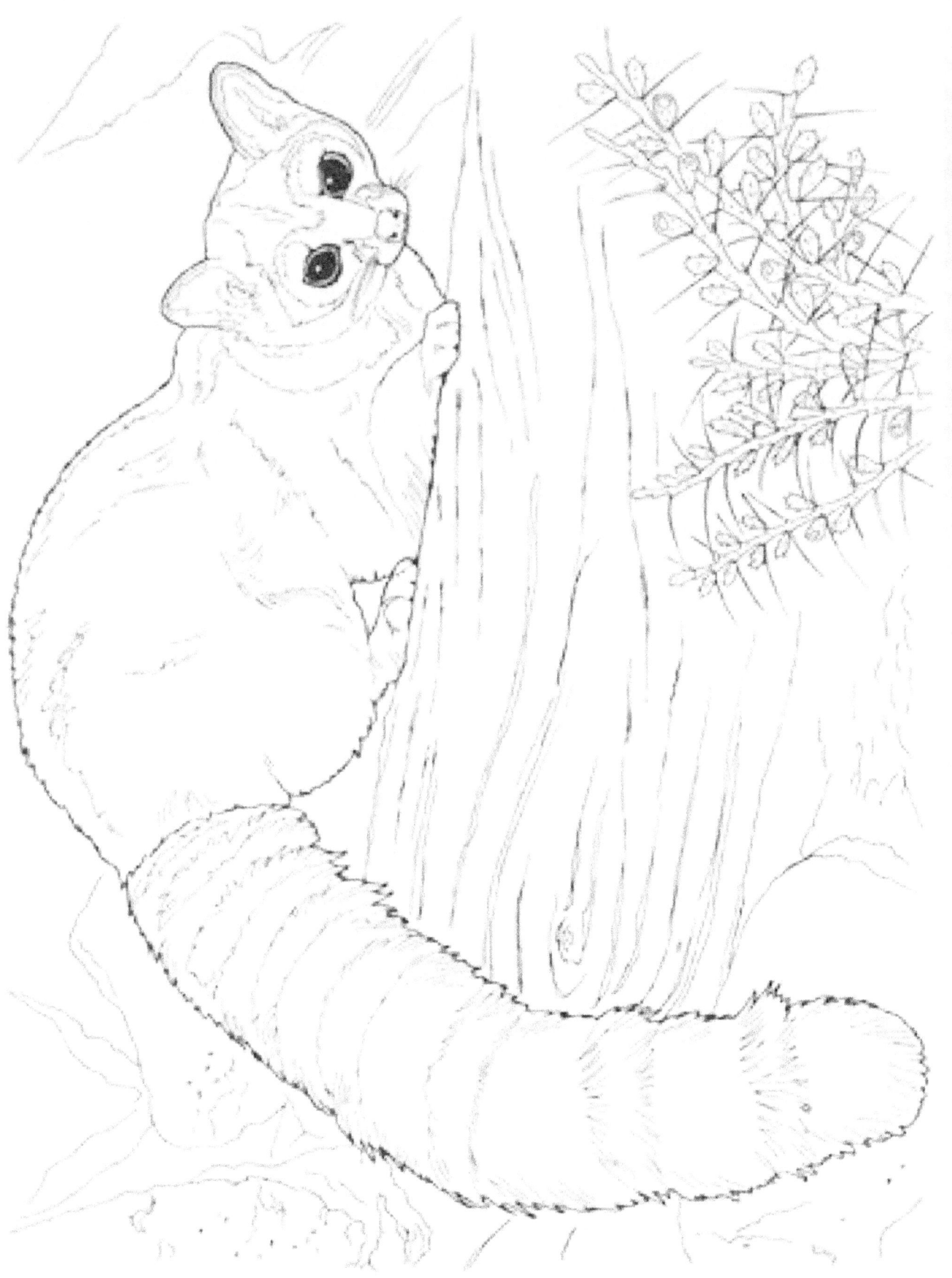

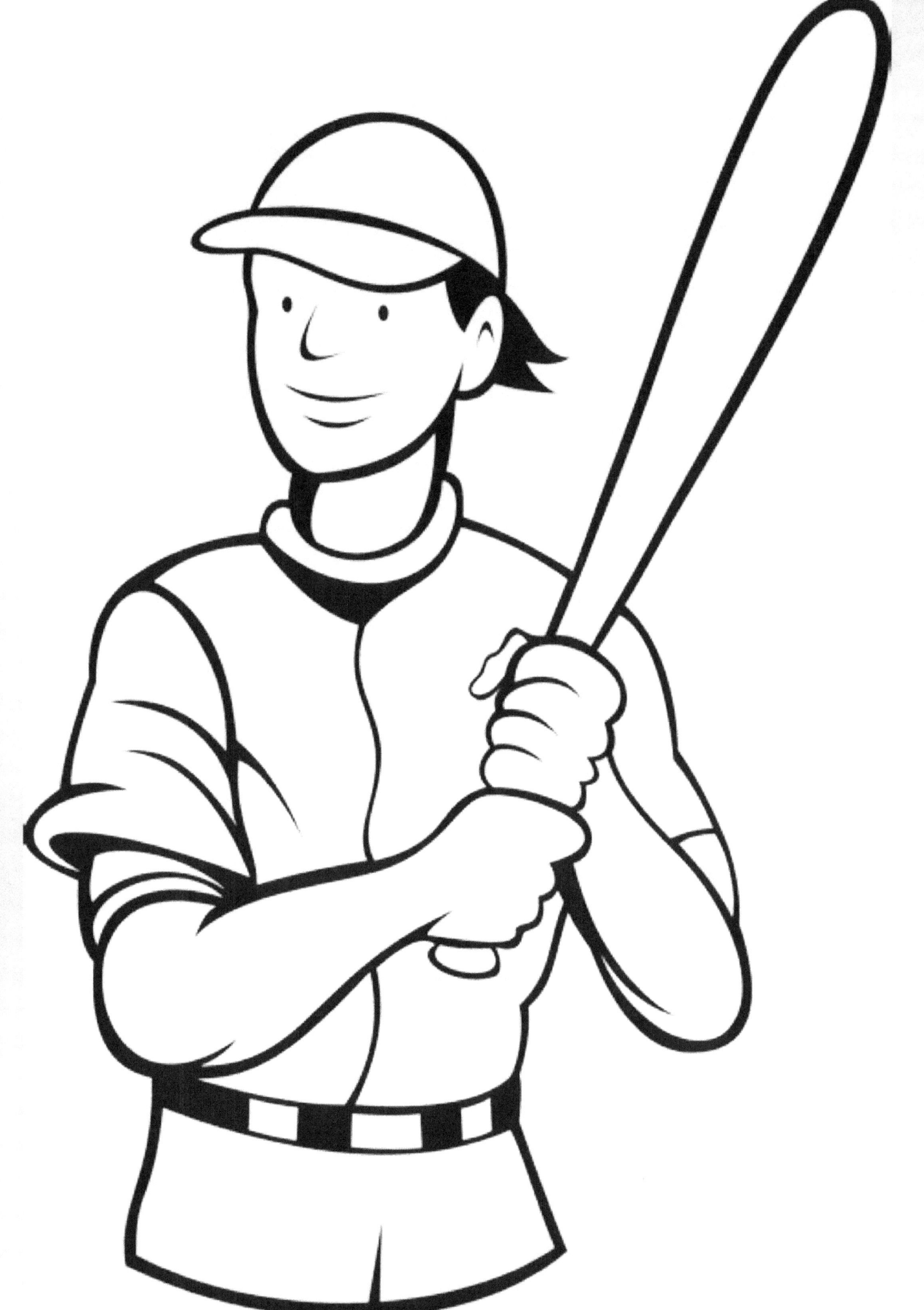

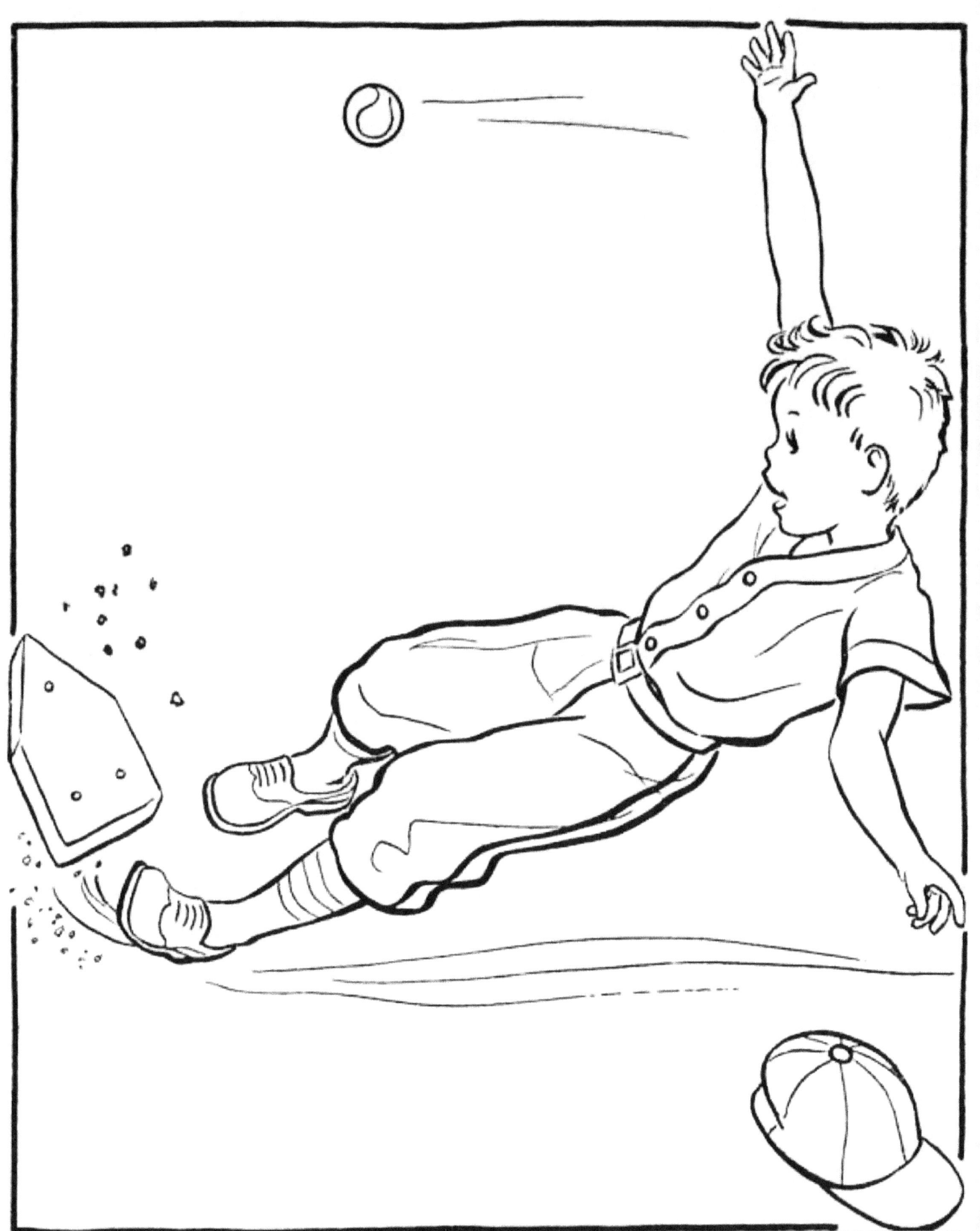

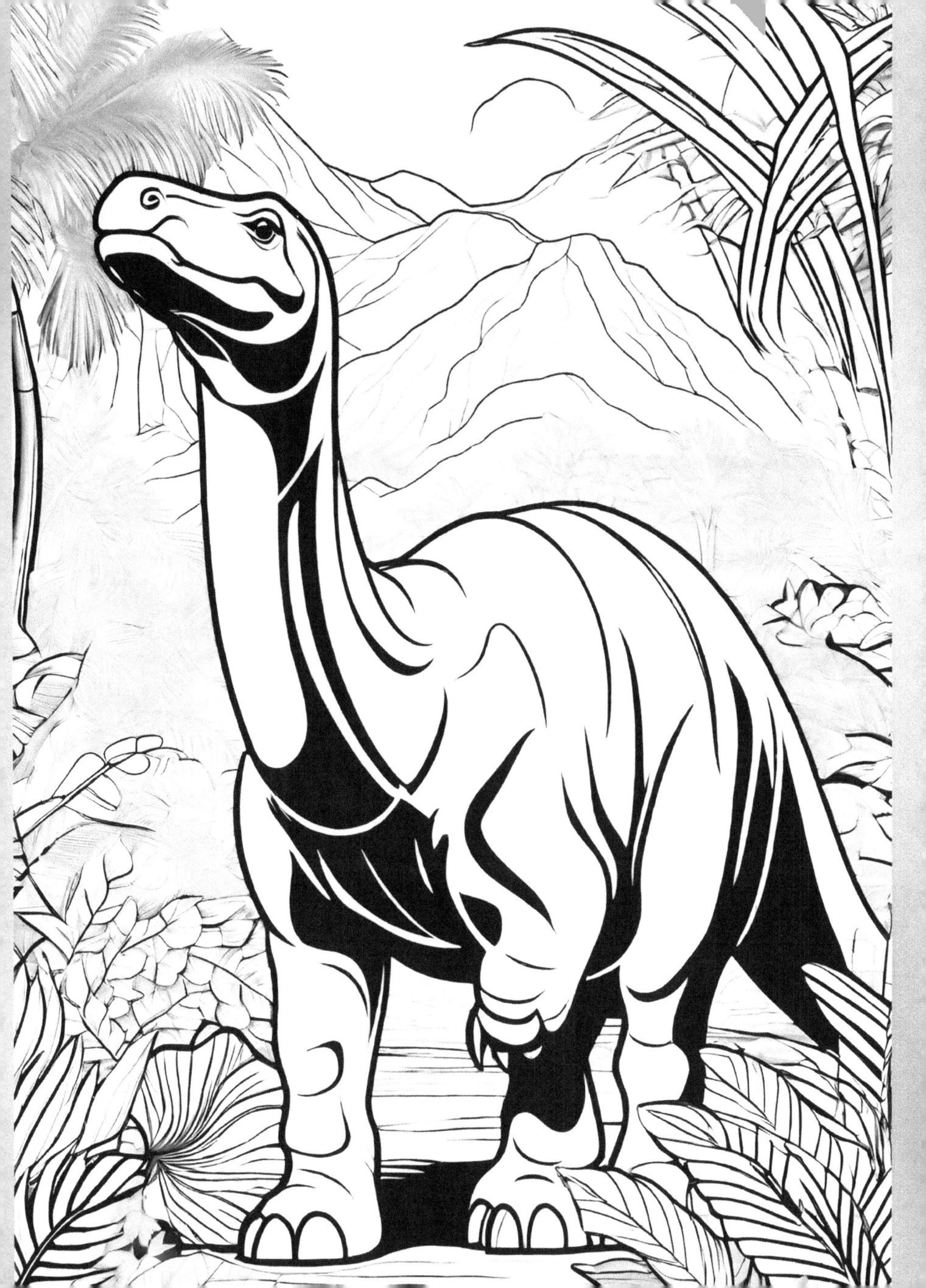

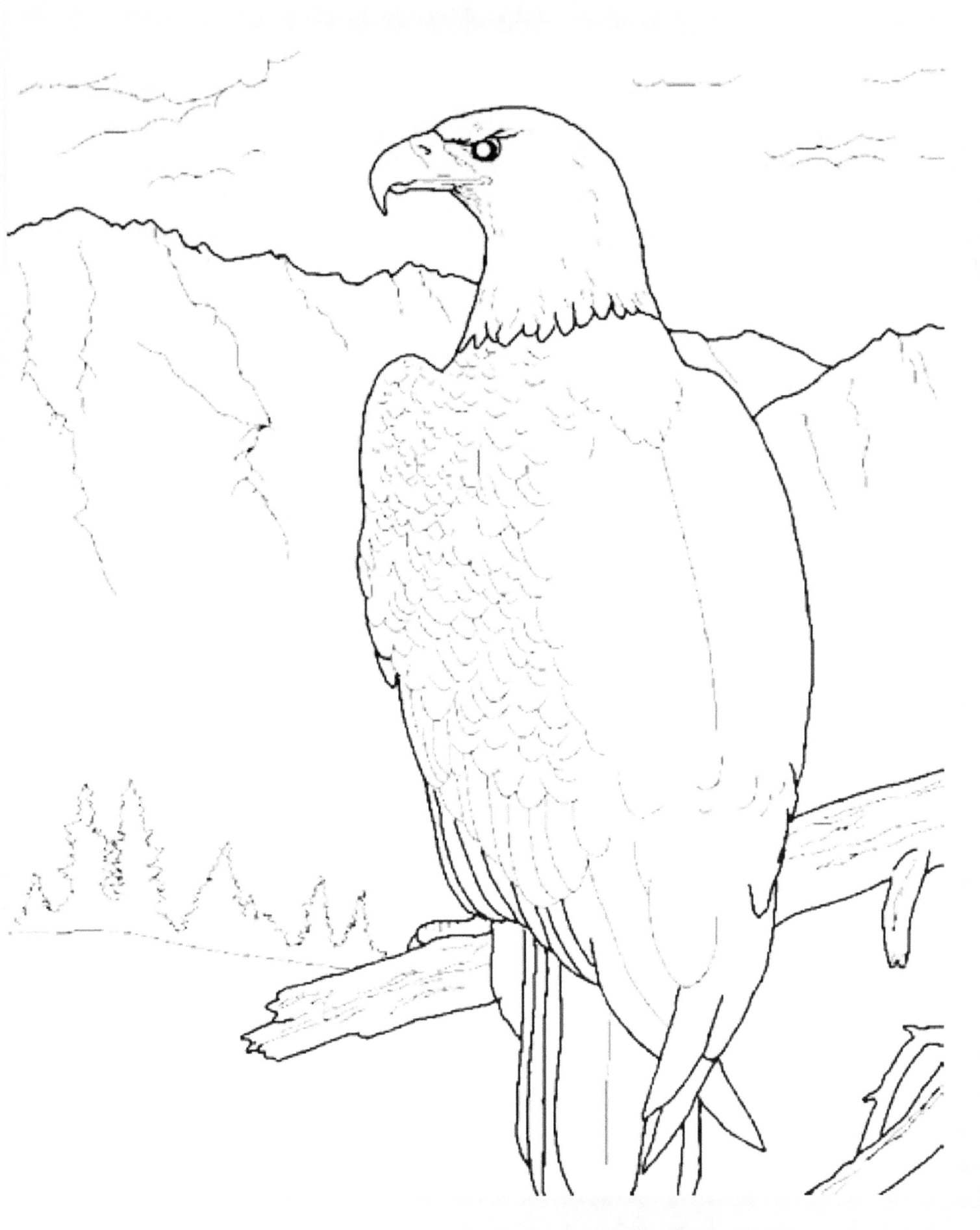

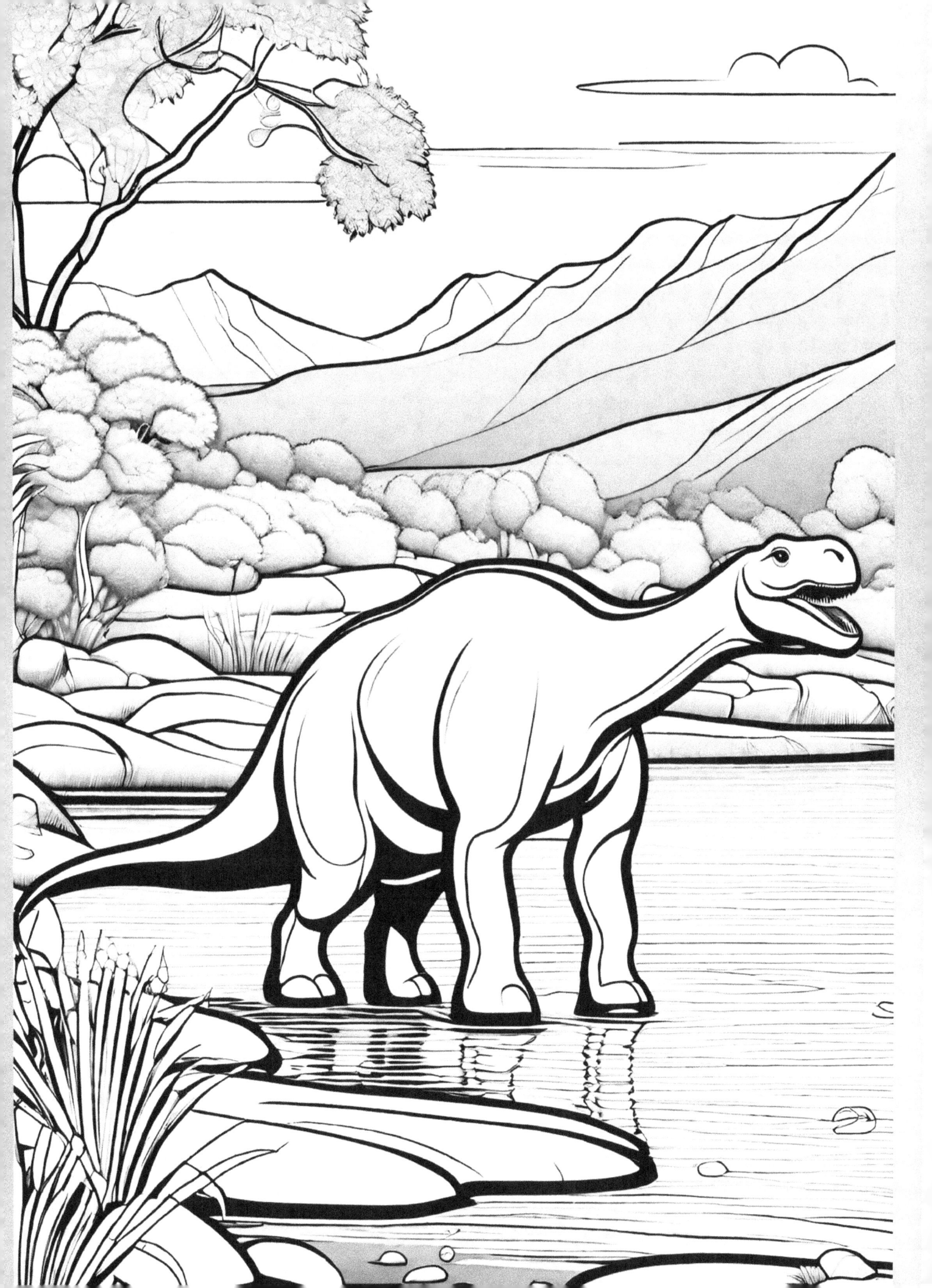

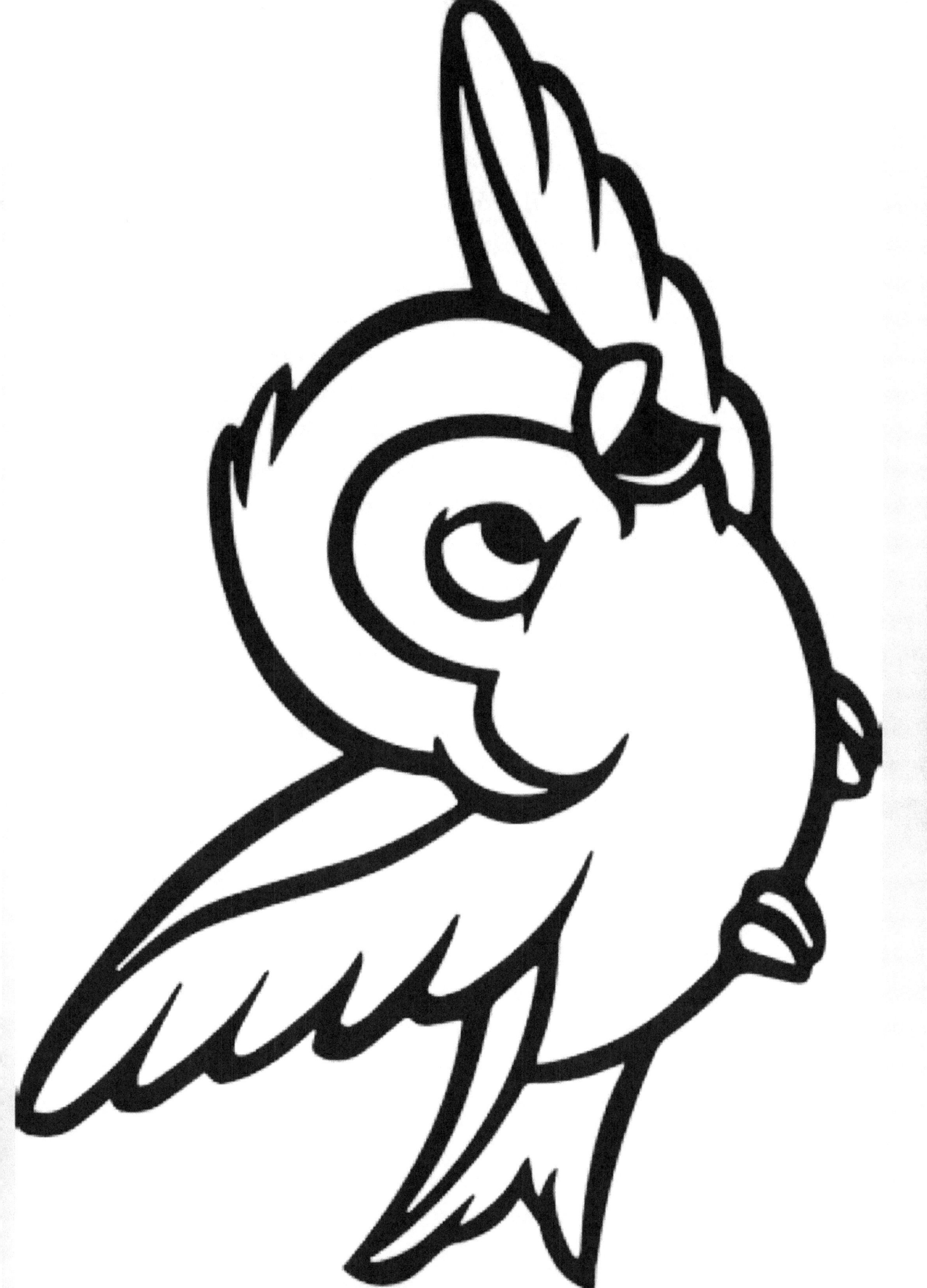

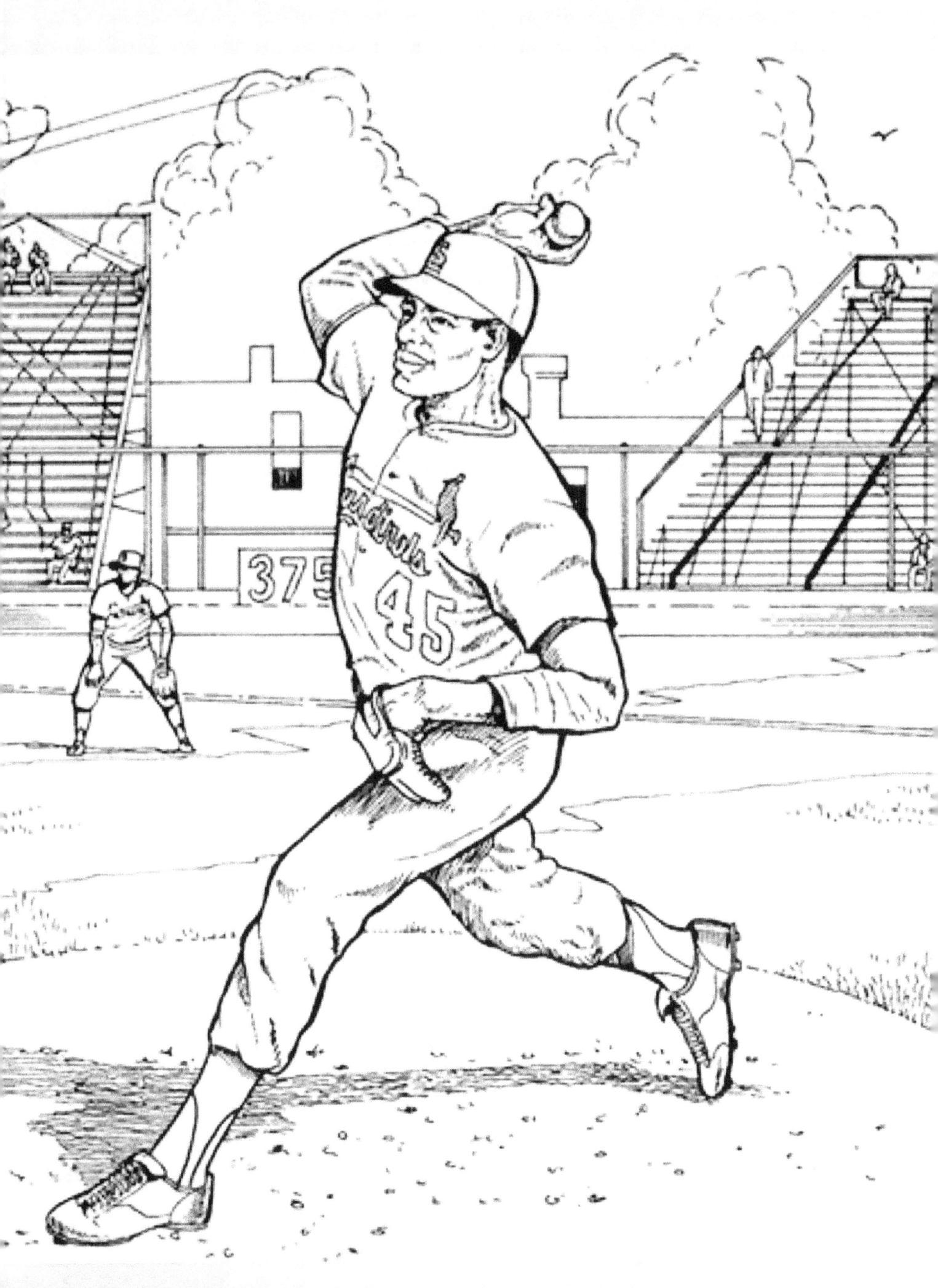

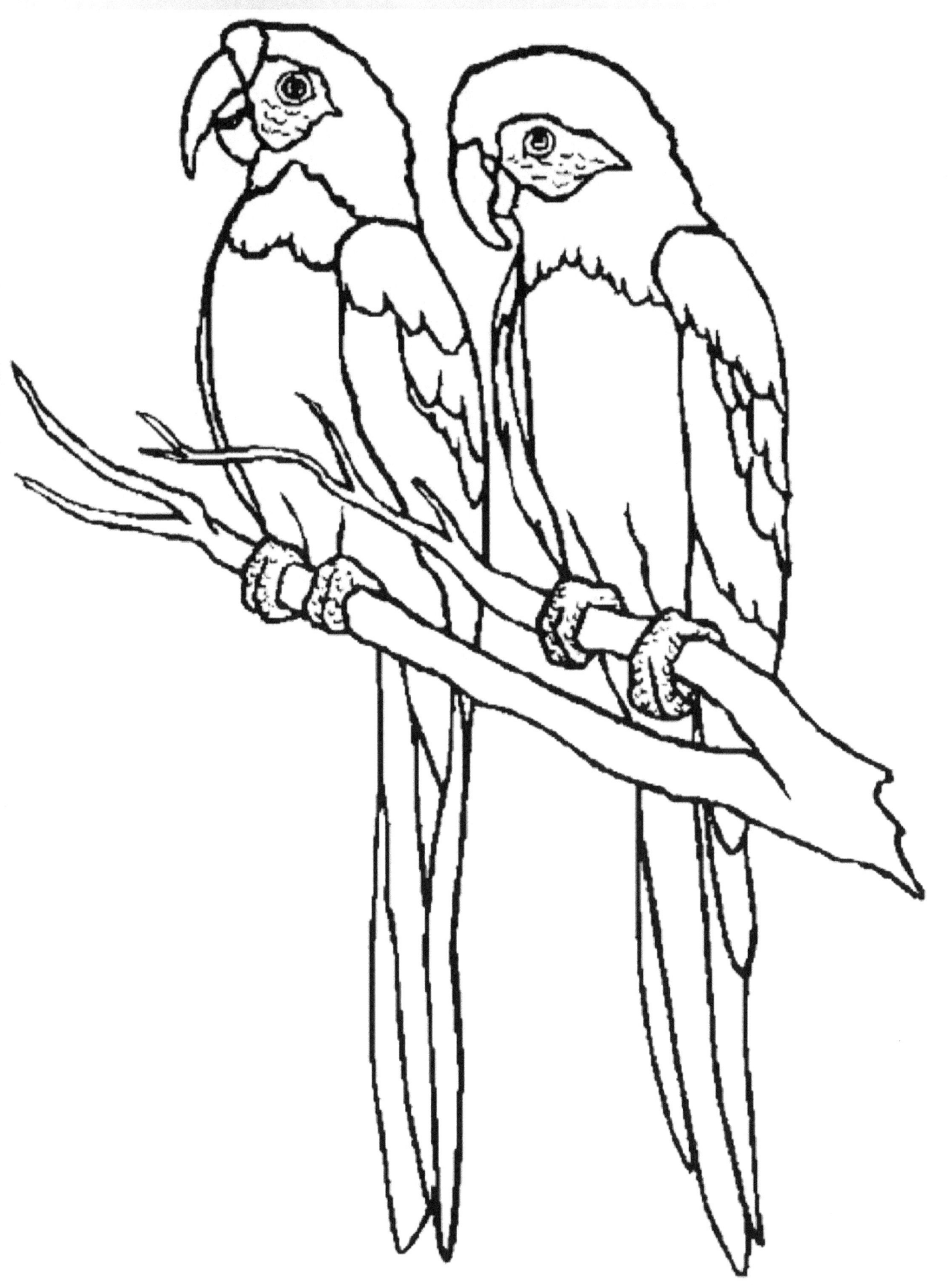

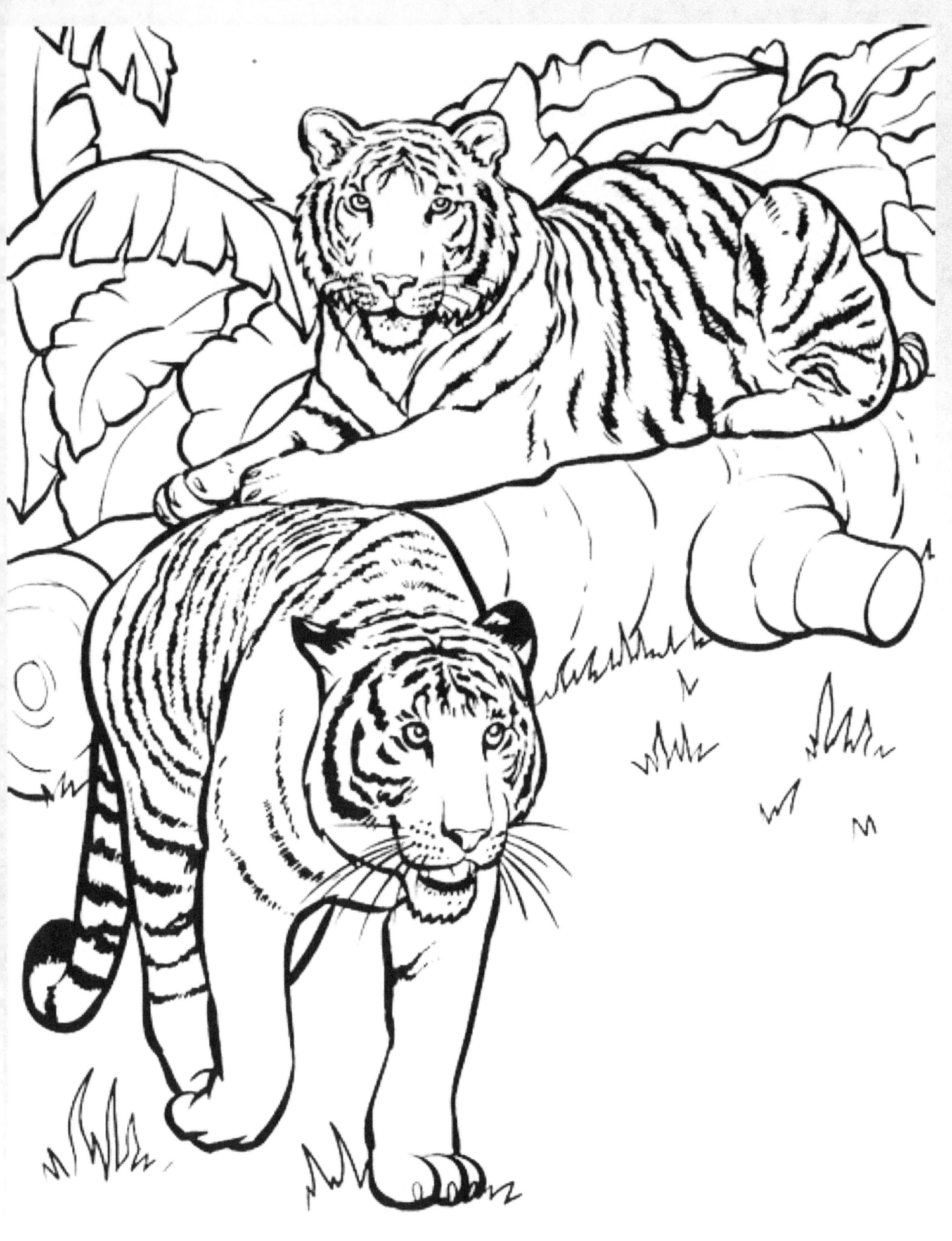

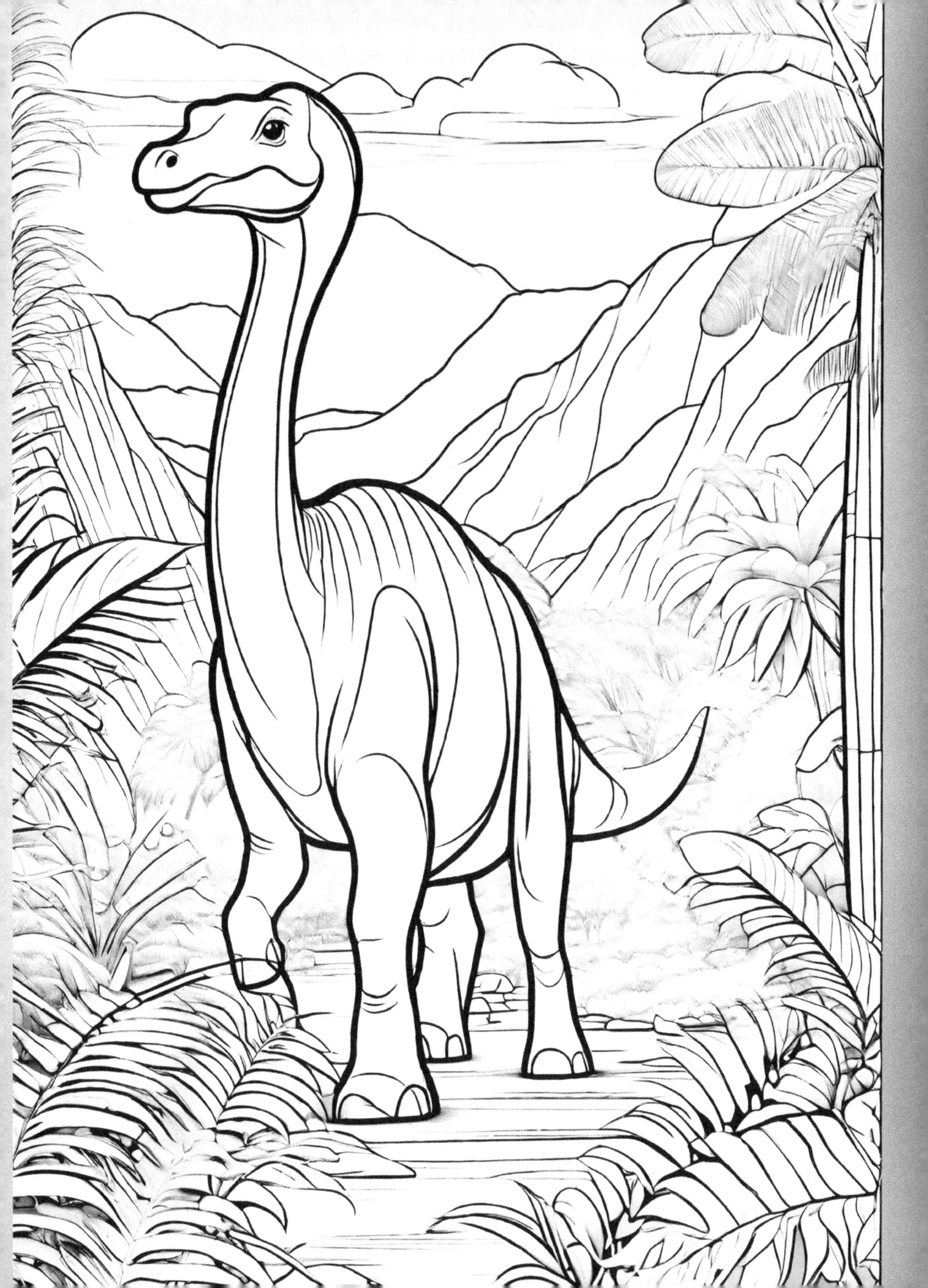

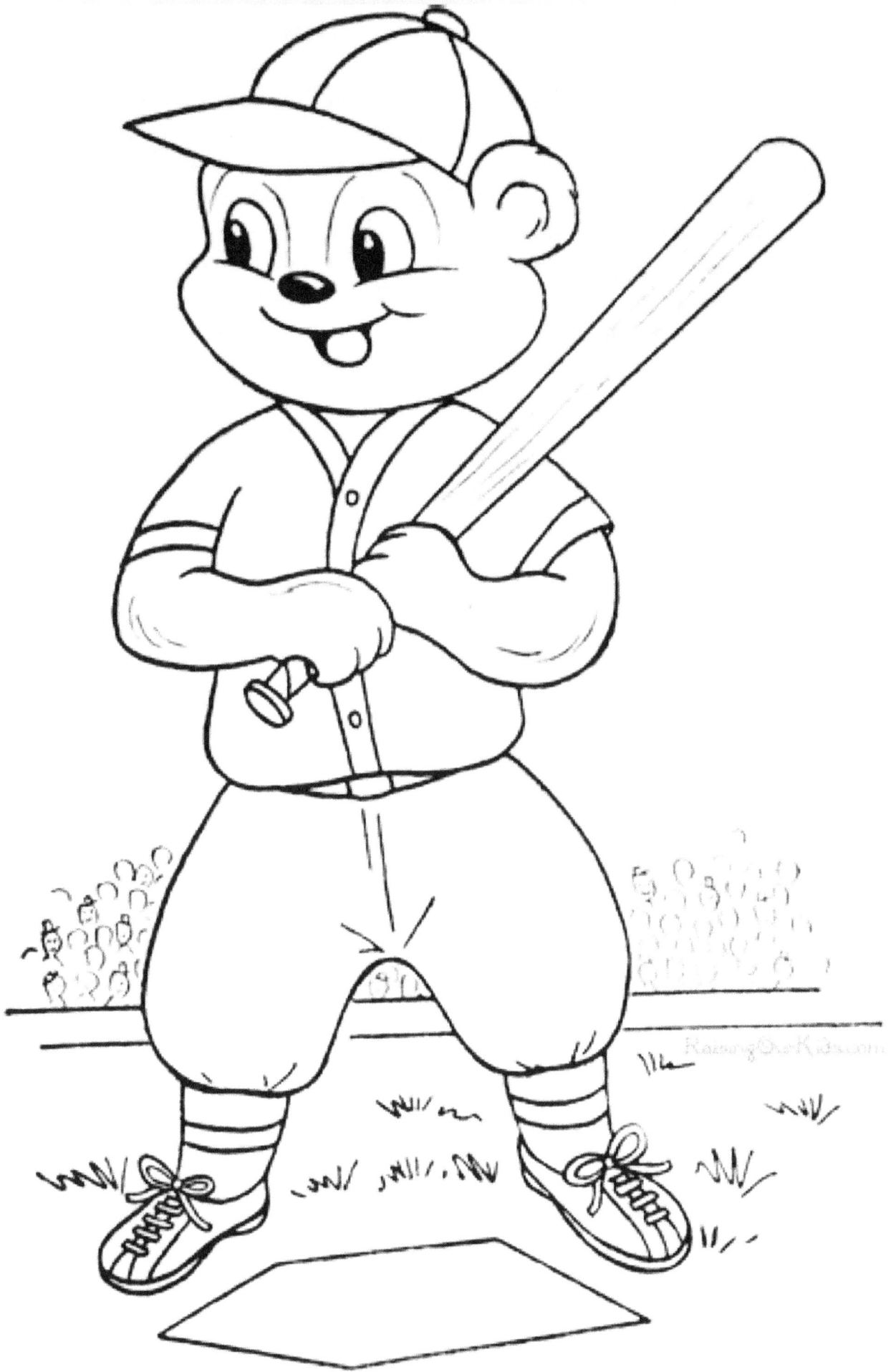

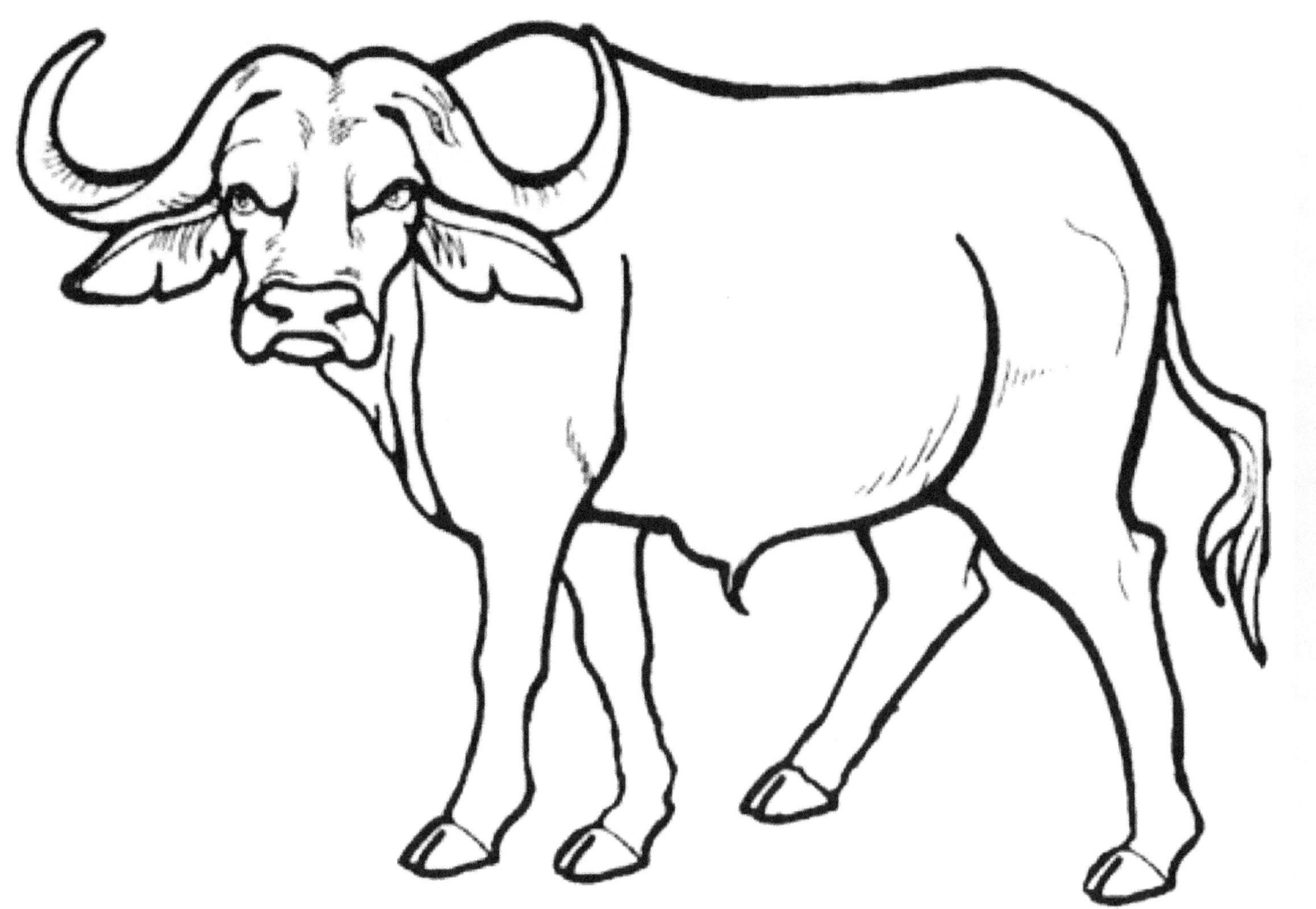

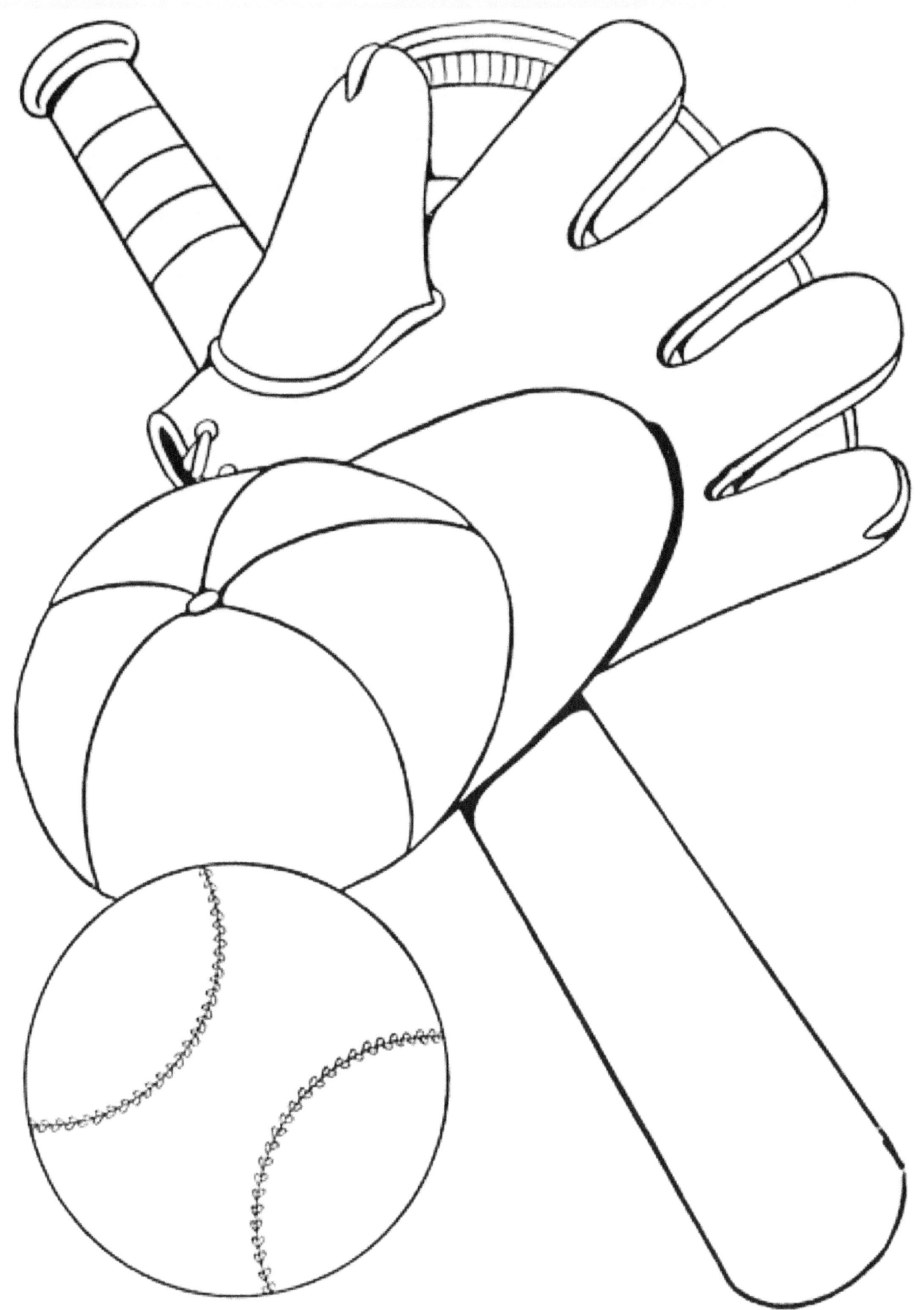

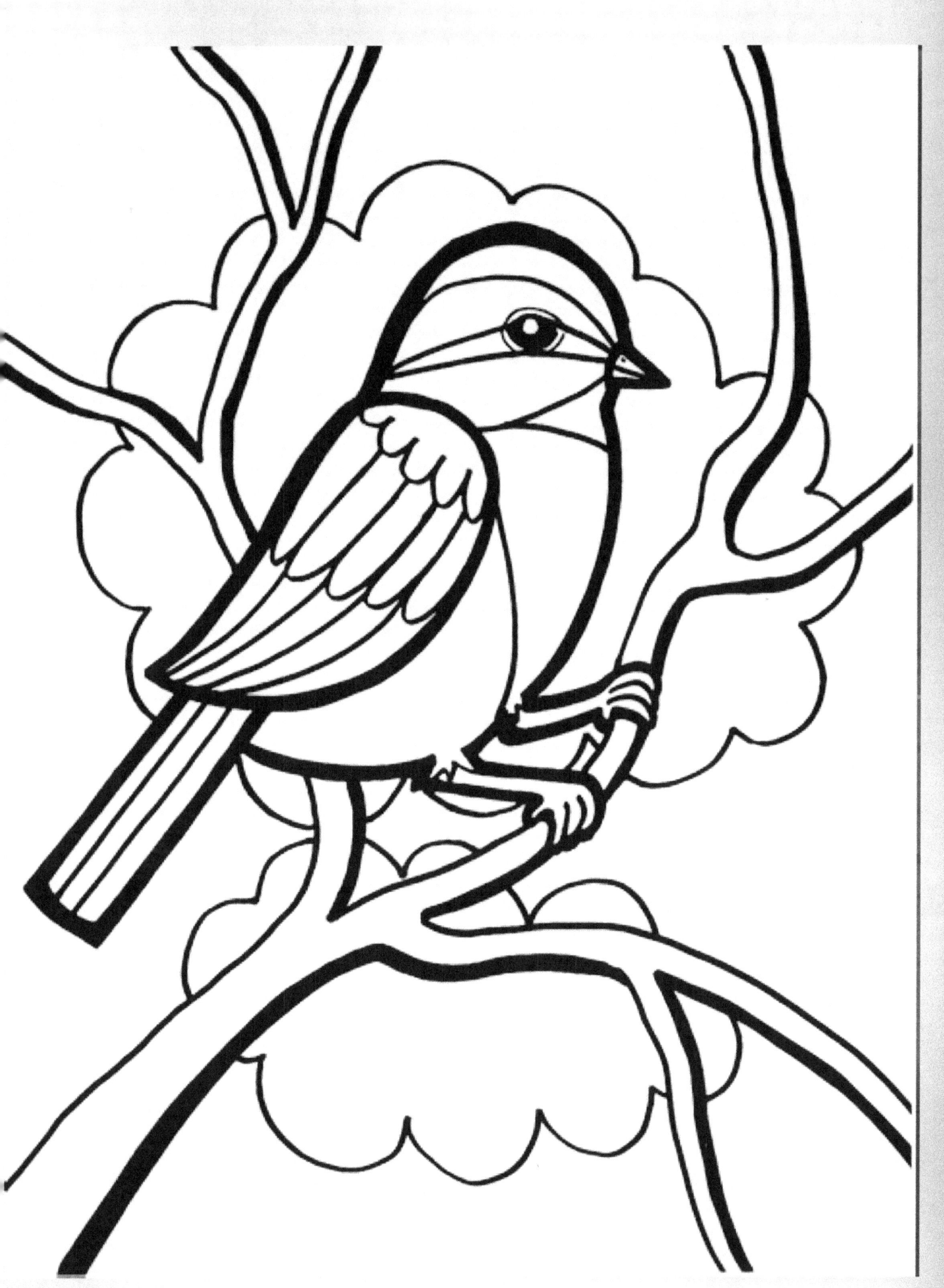

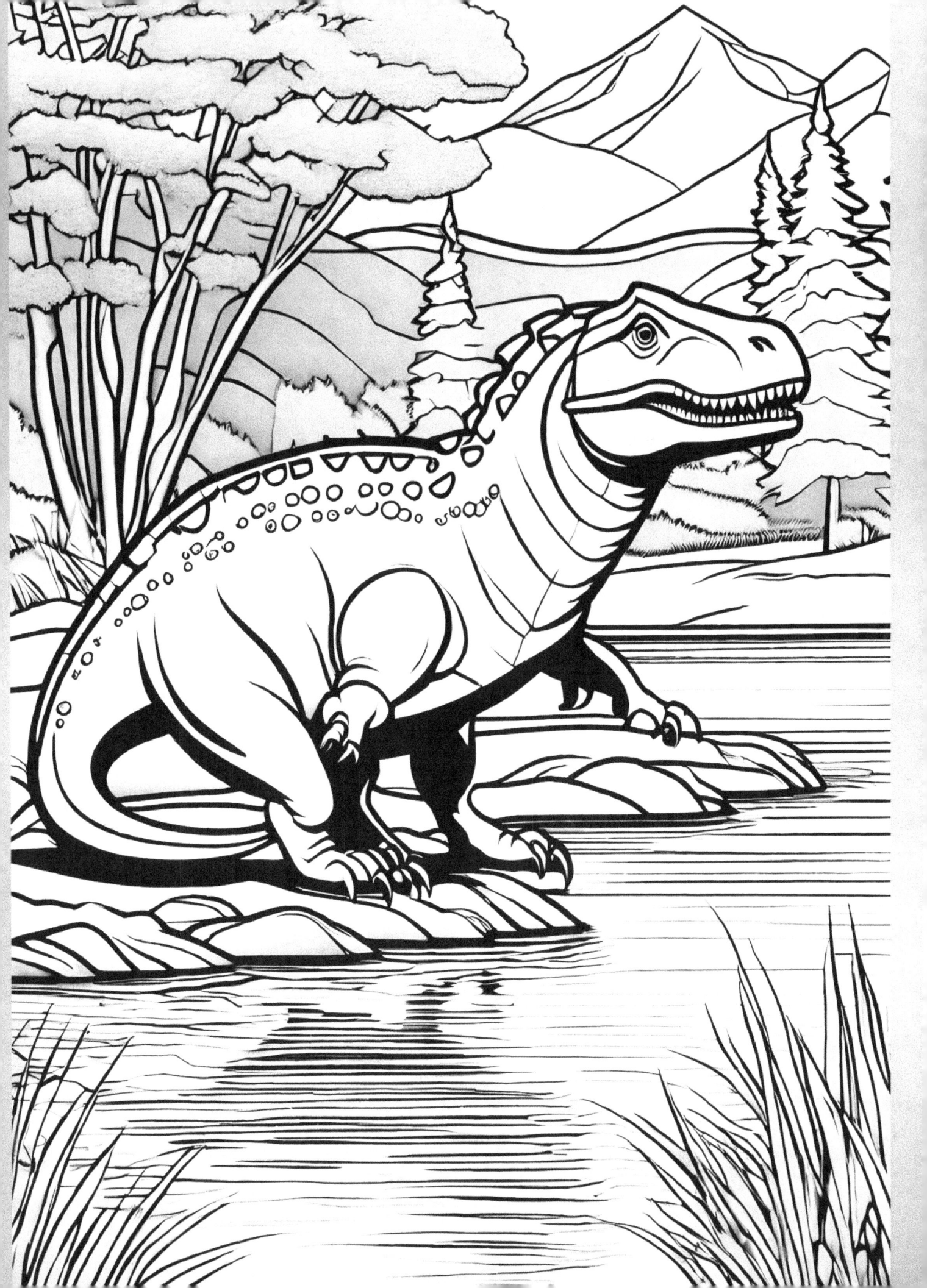

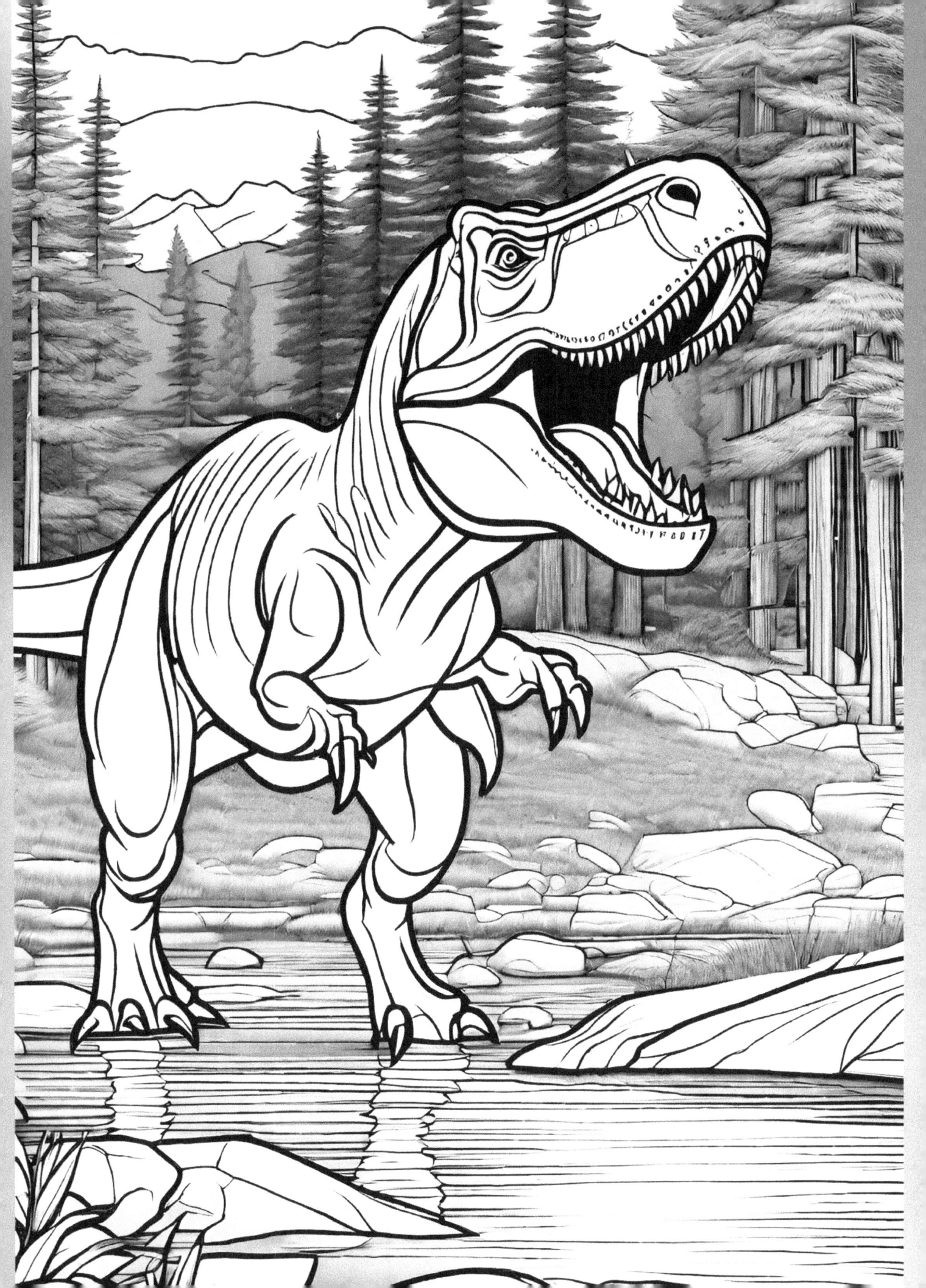

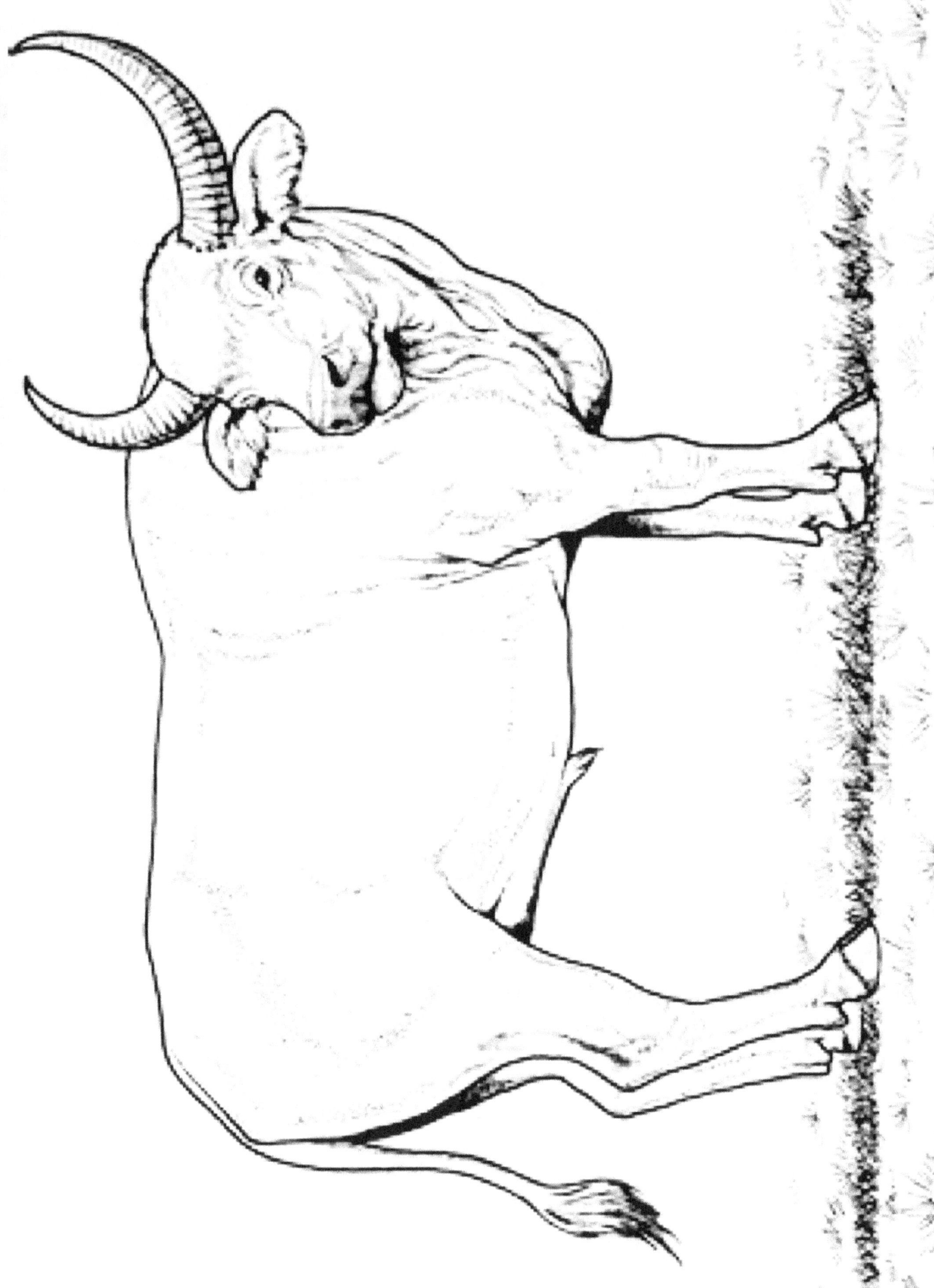

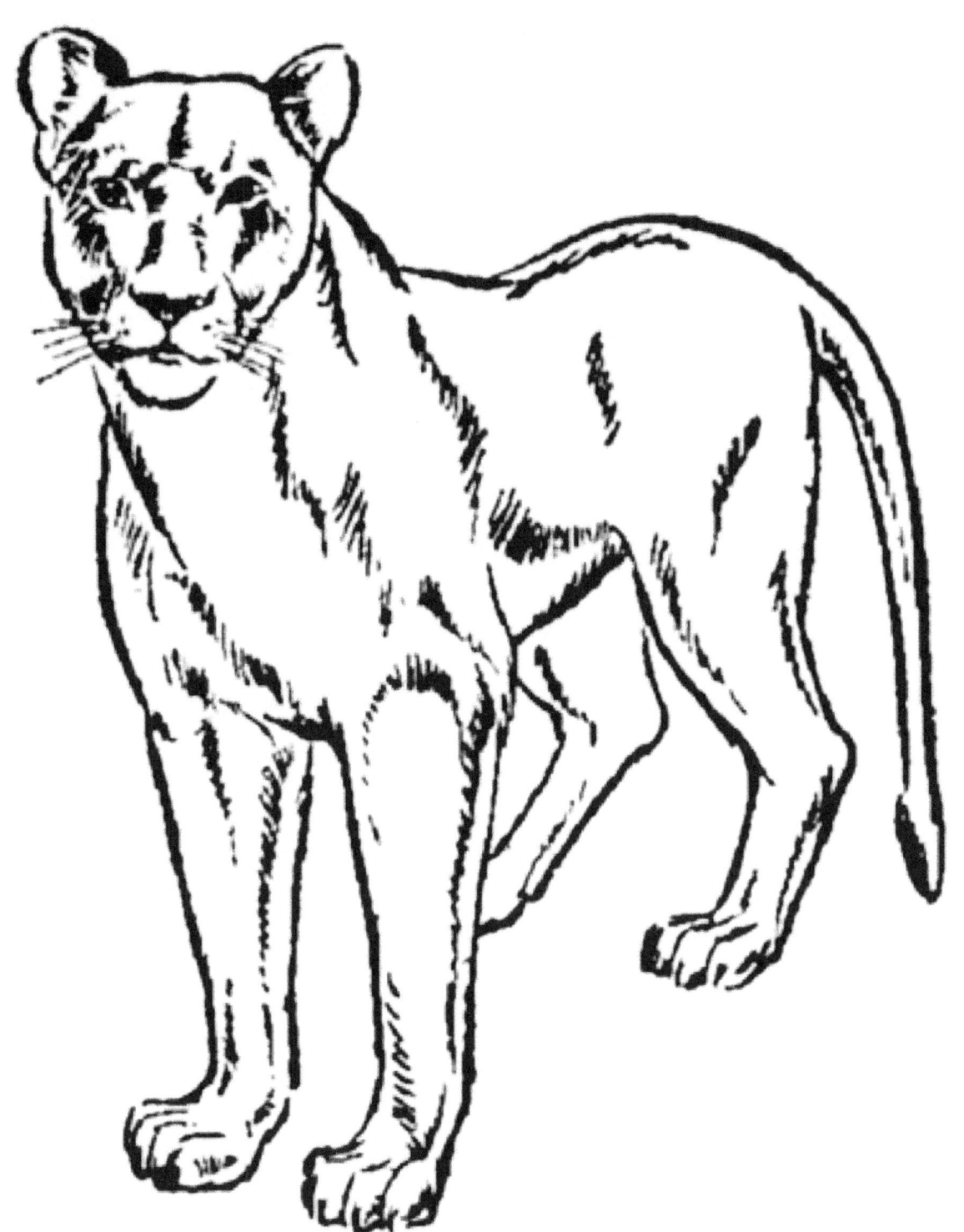

LION
Golden-tan

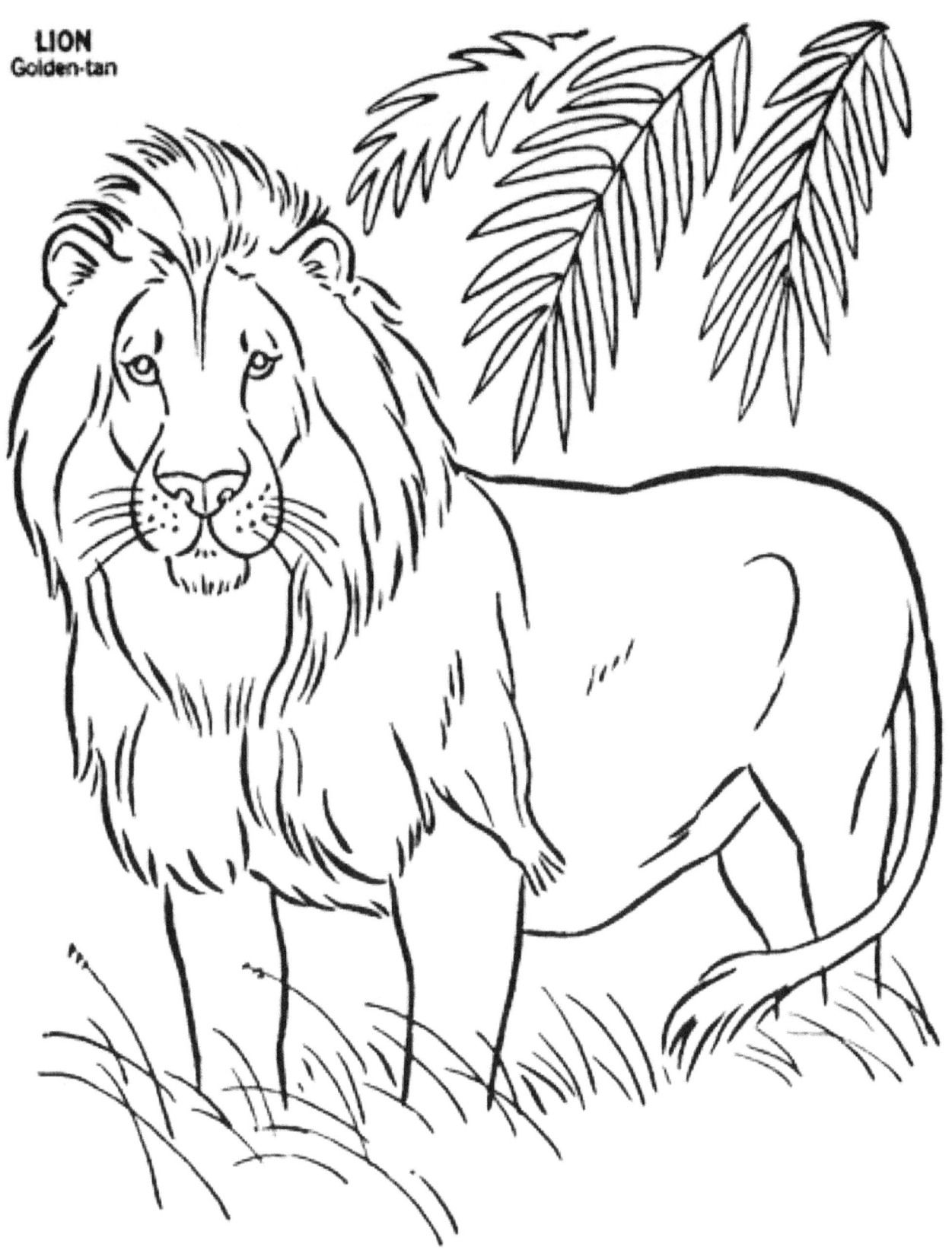

The king of animals prefers deserts and plains to the jungles.

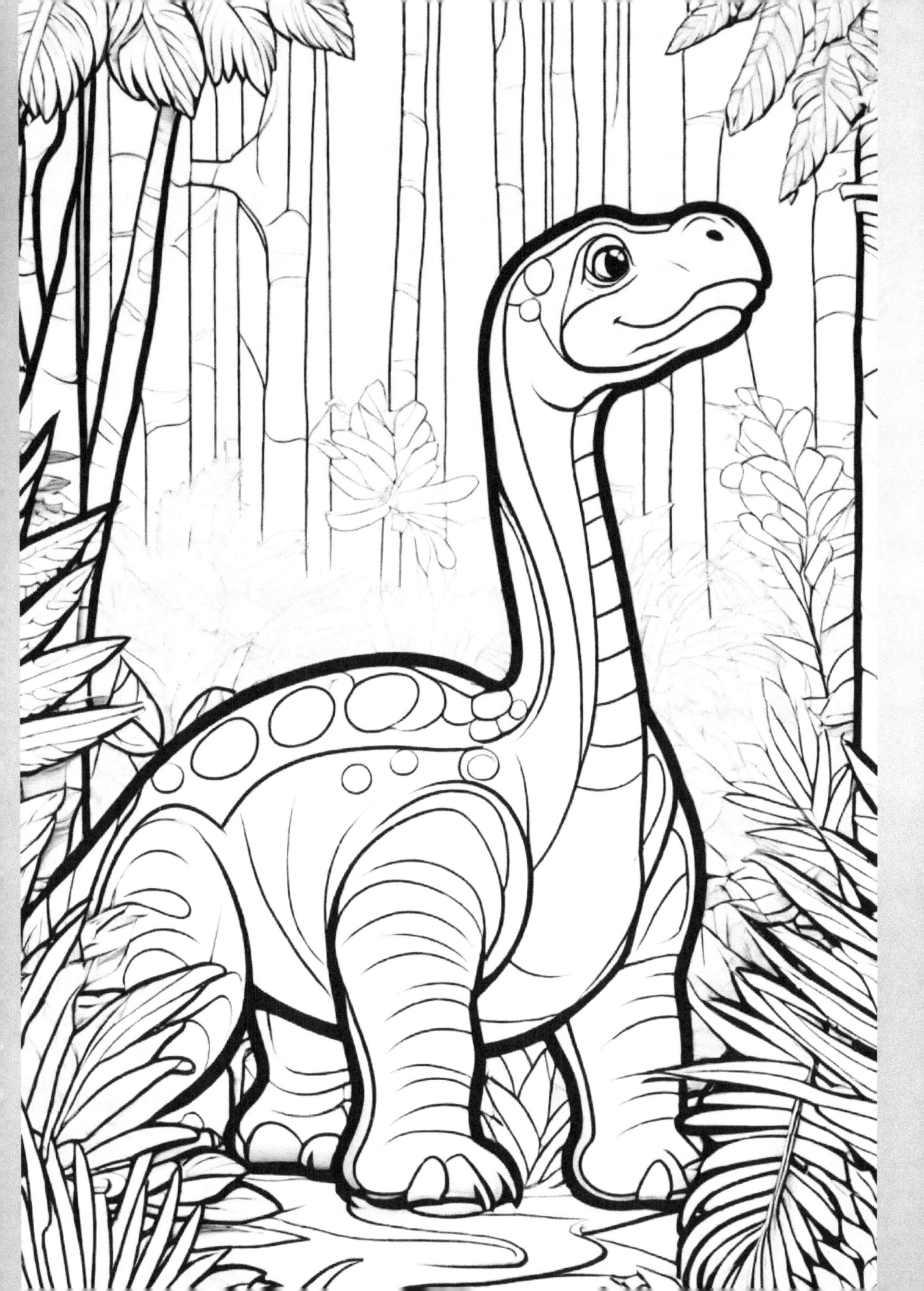

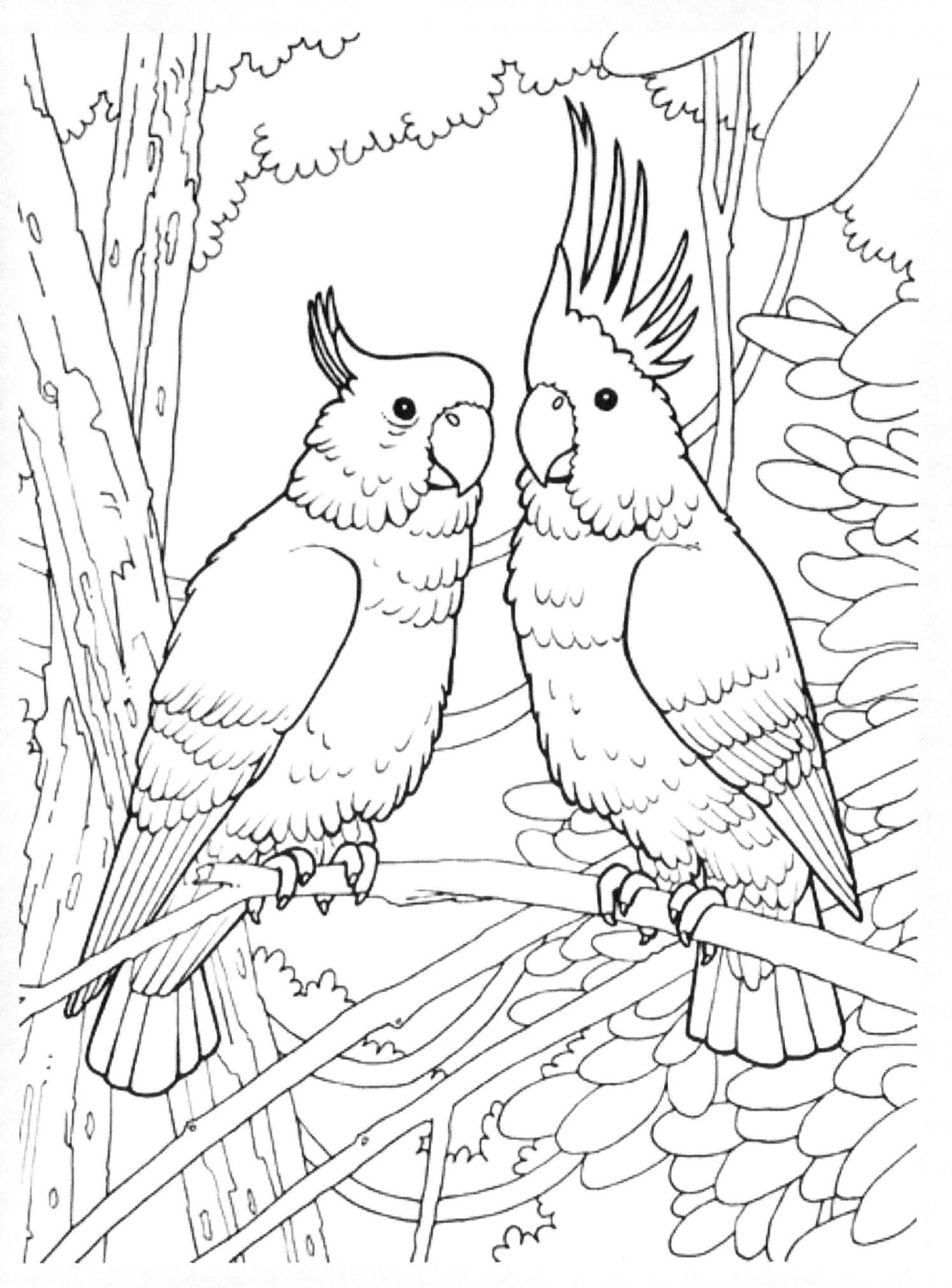

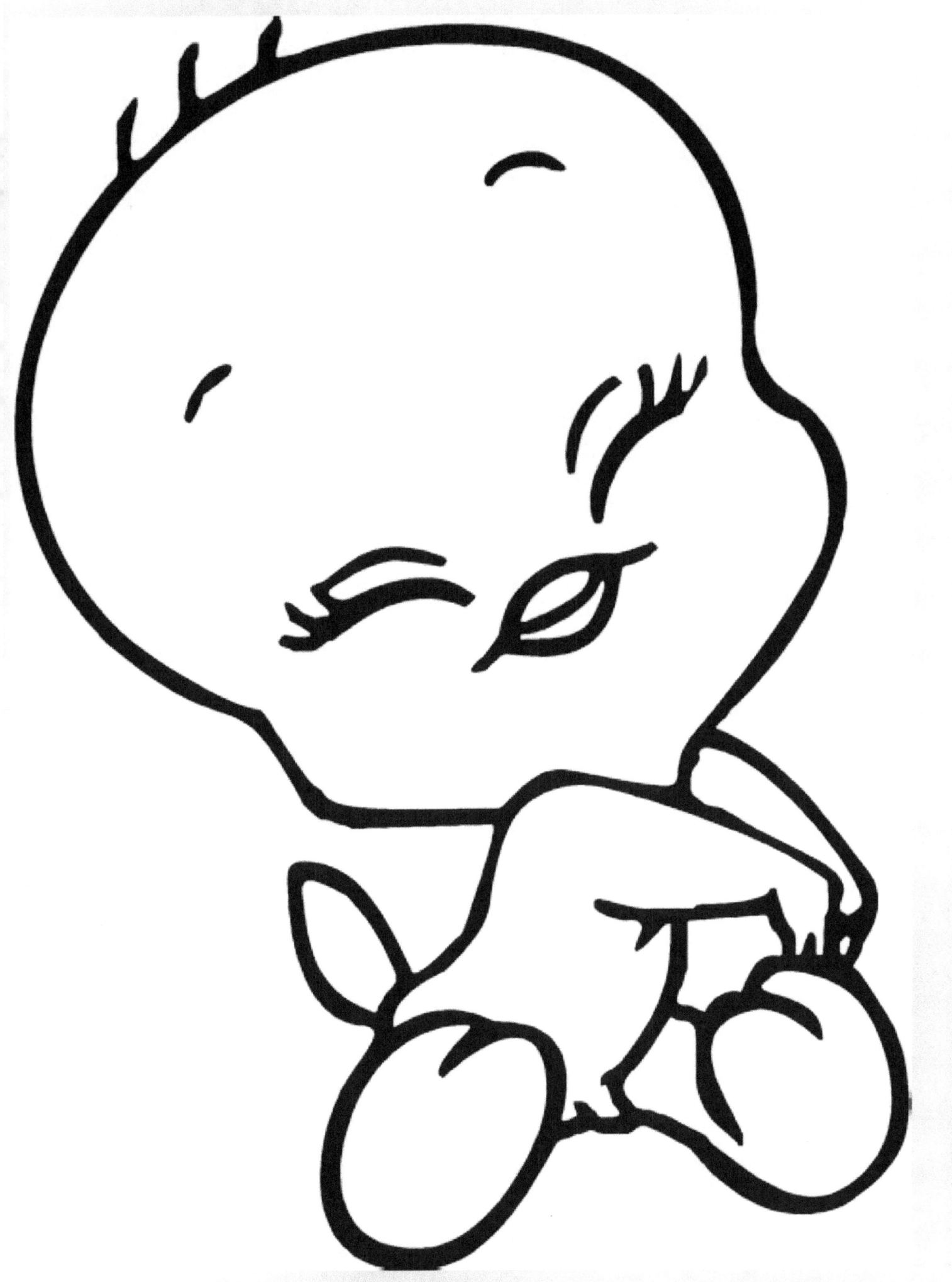

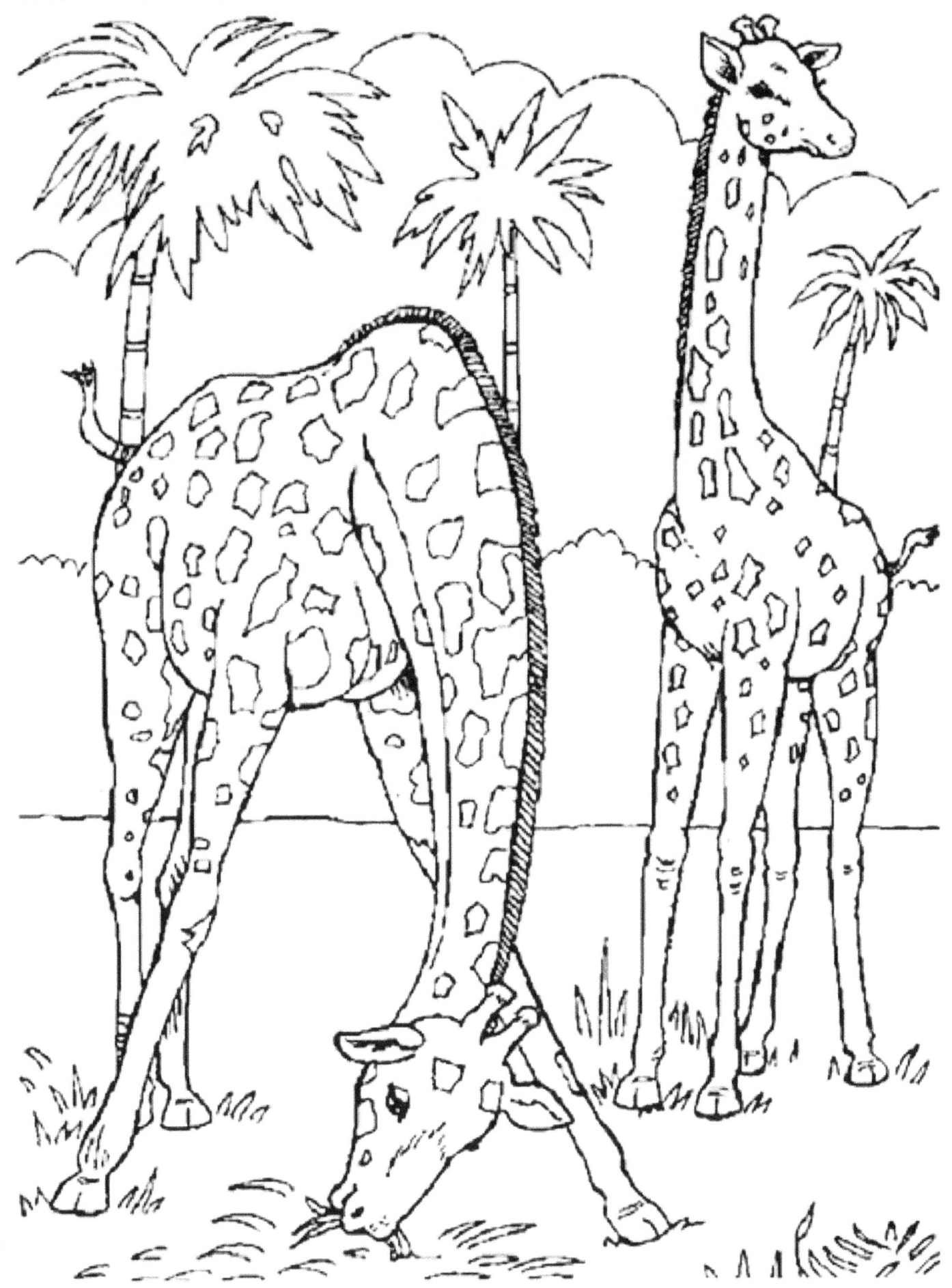

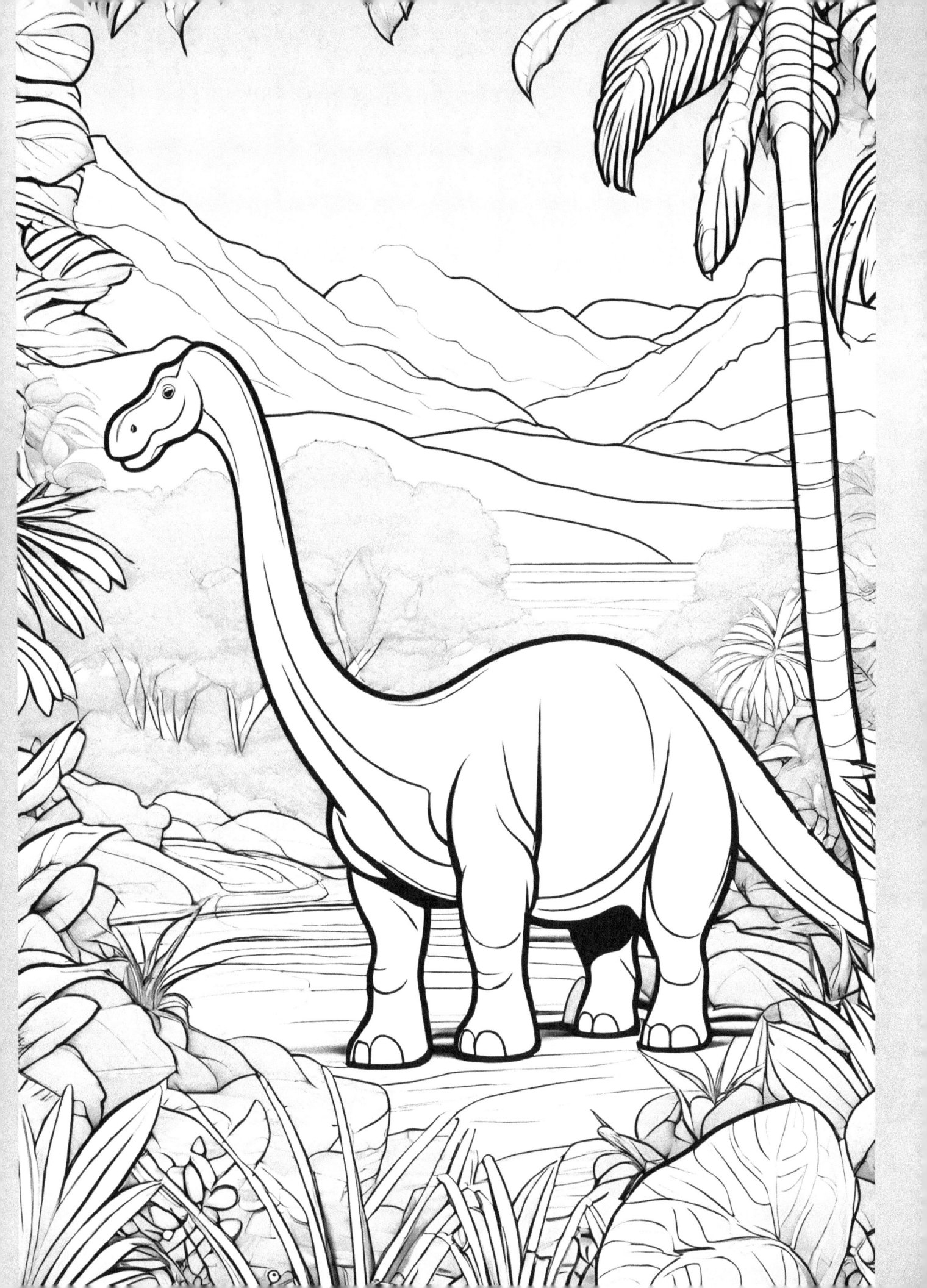

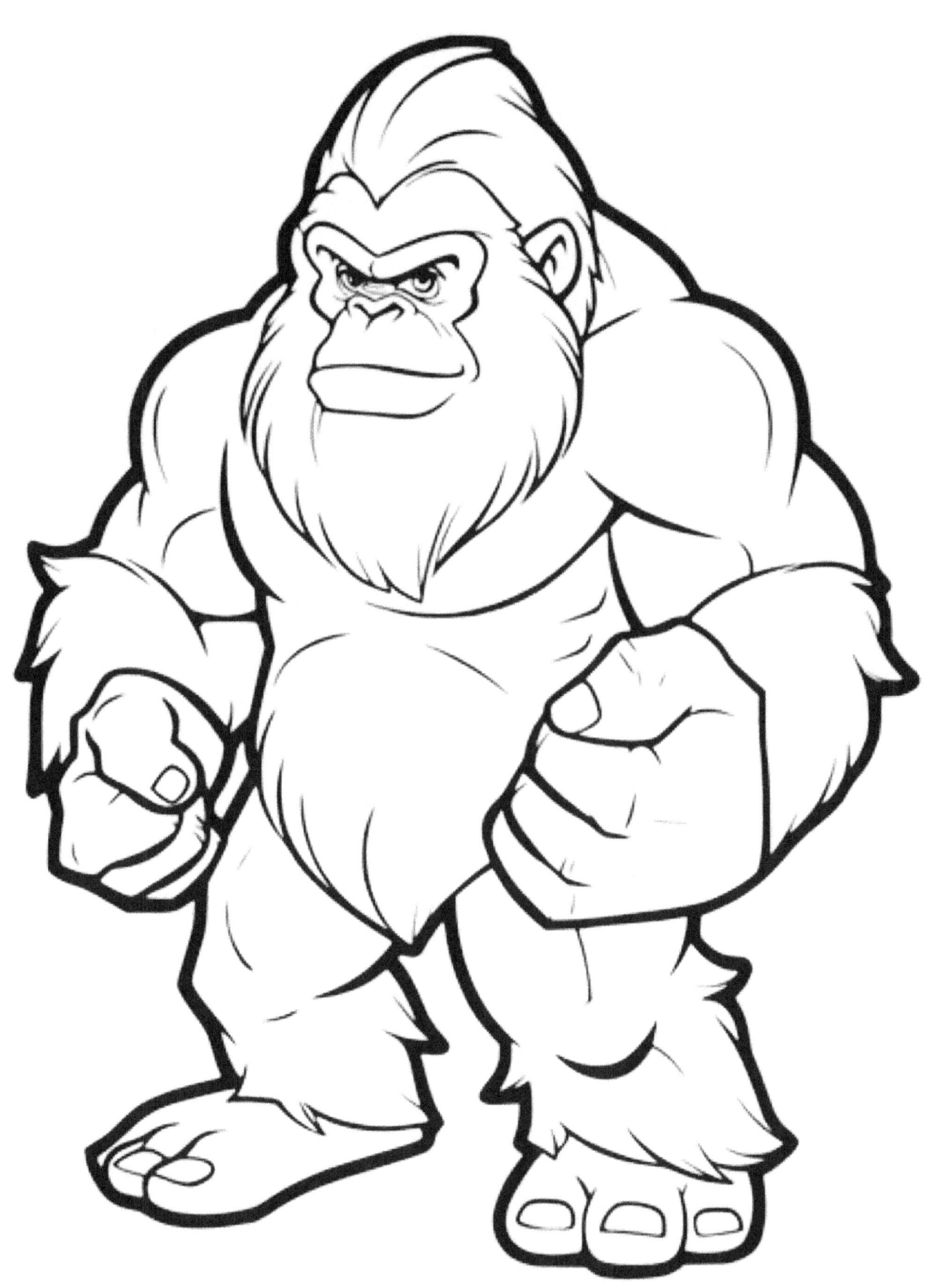

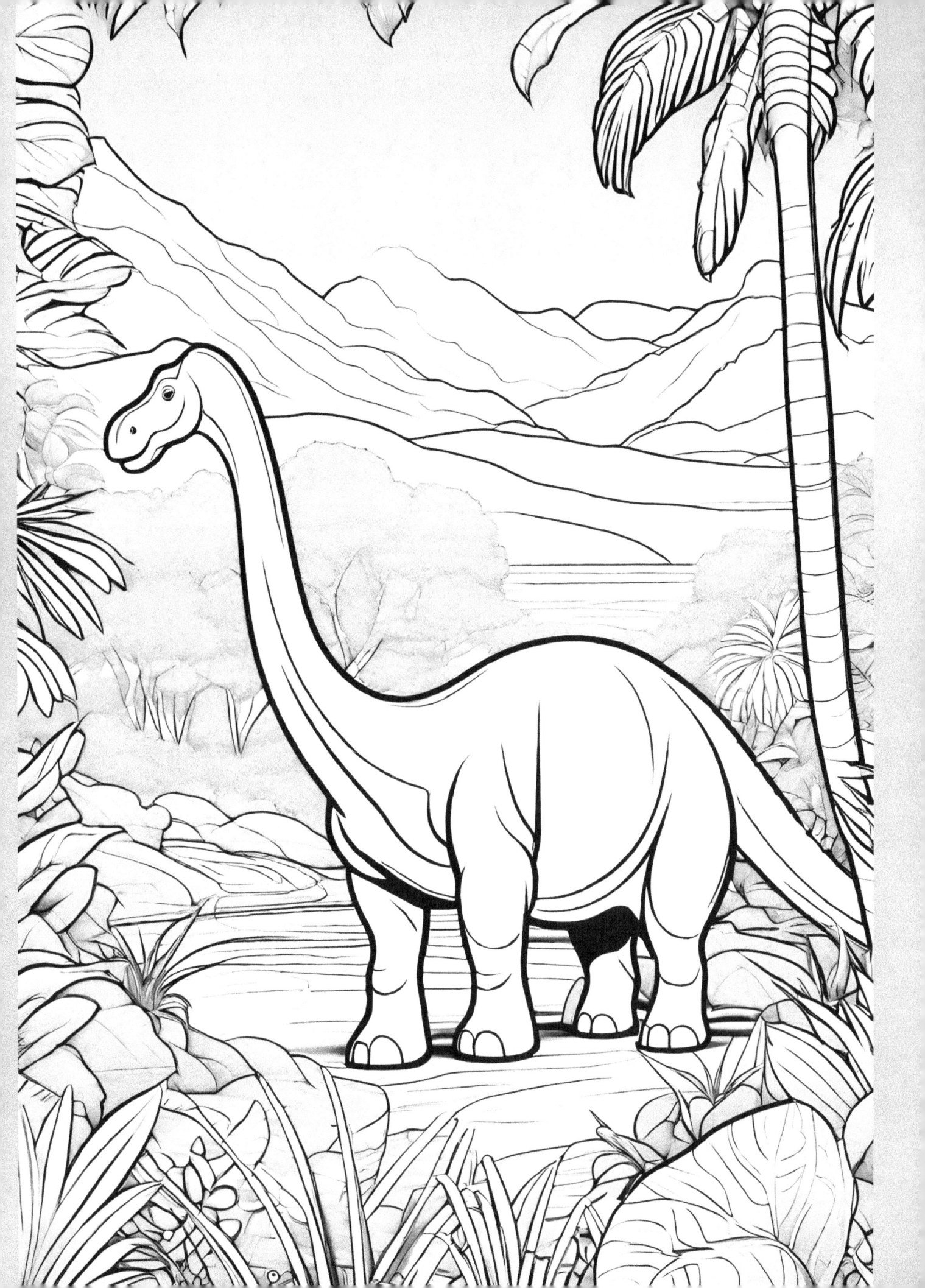

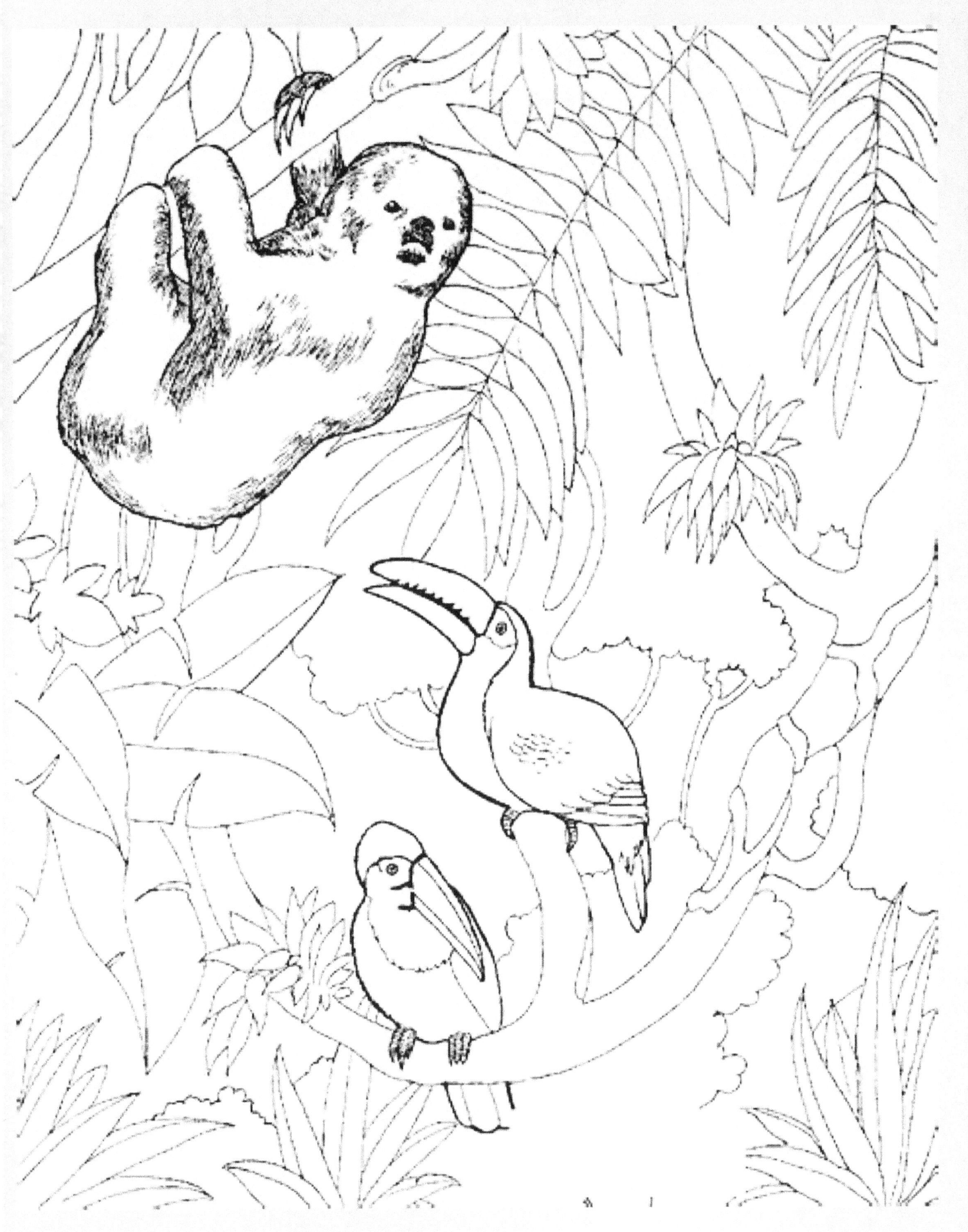

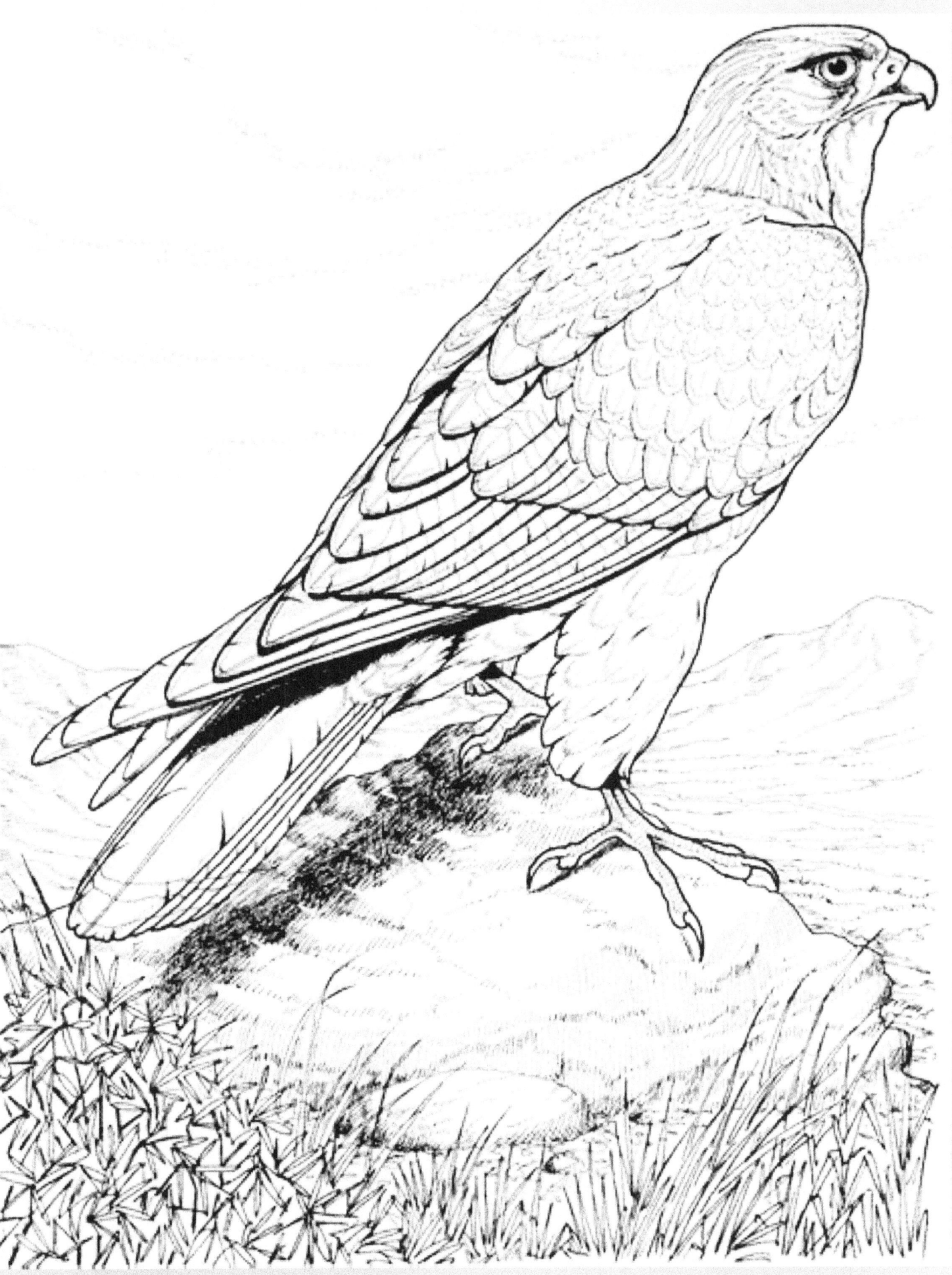

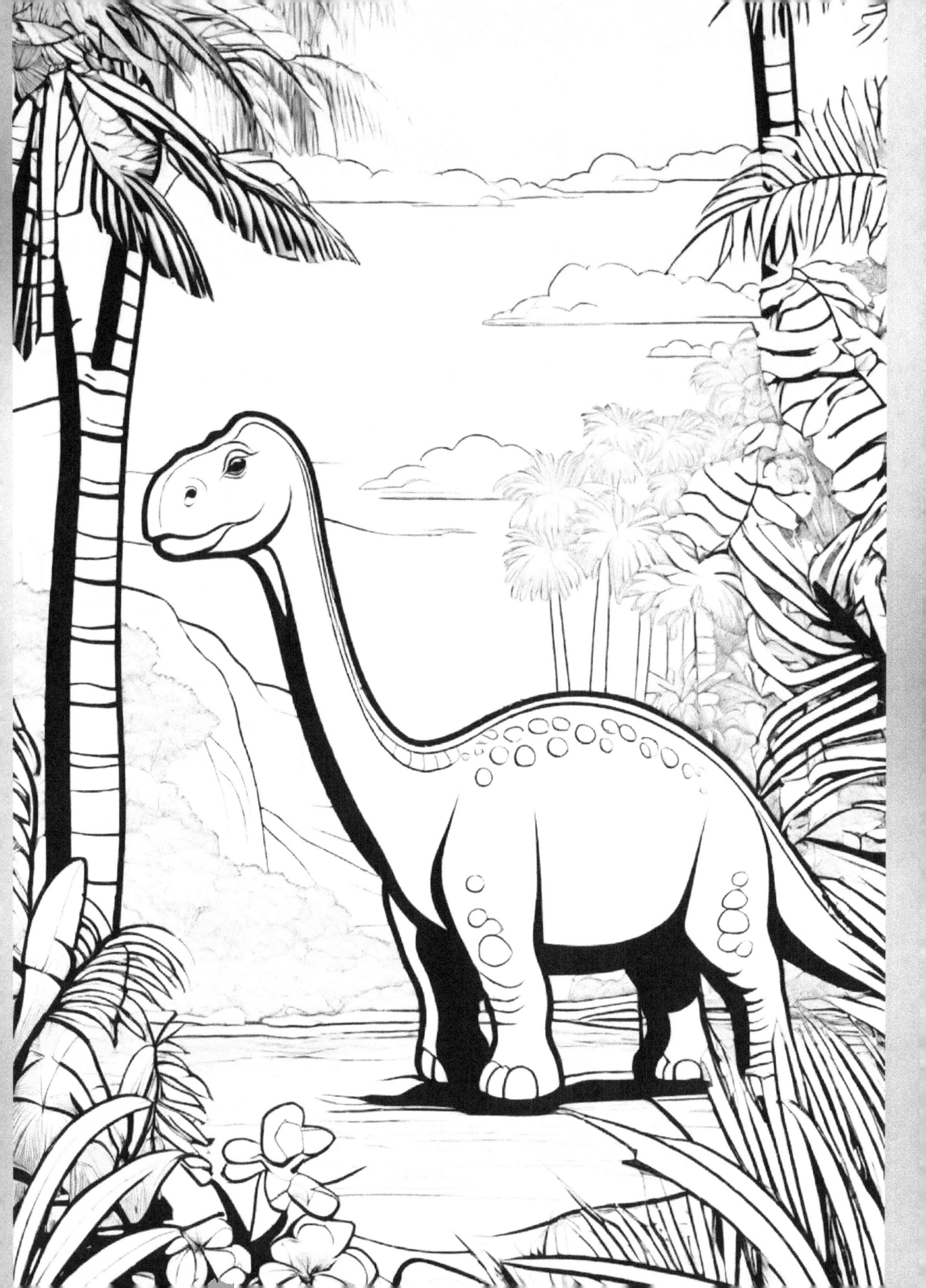

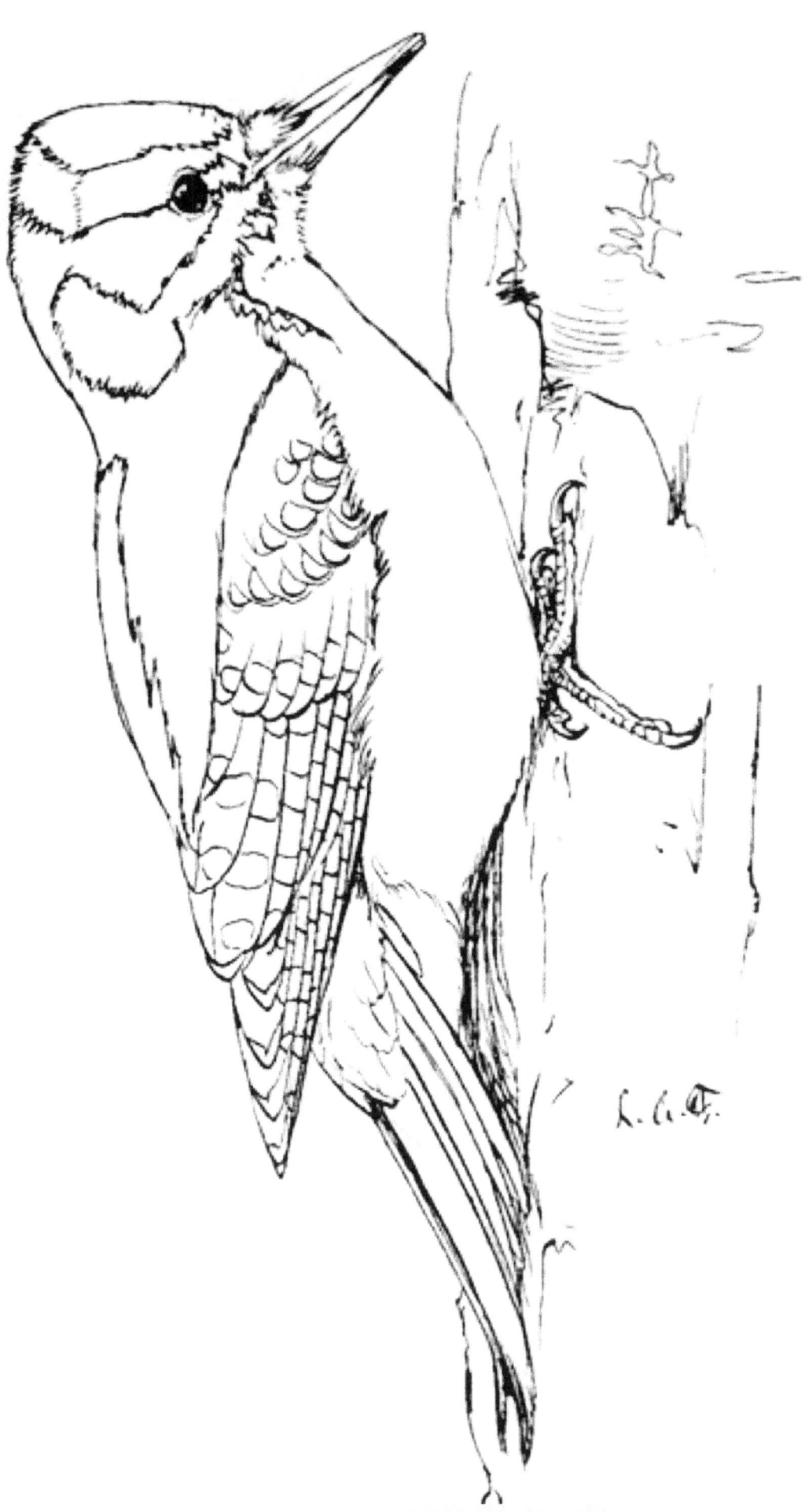

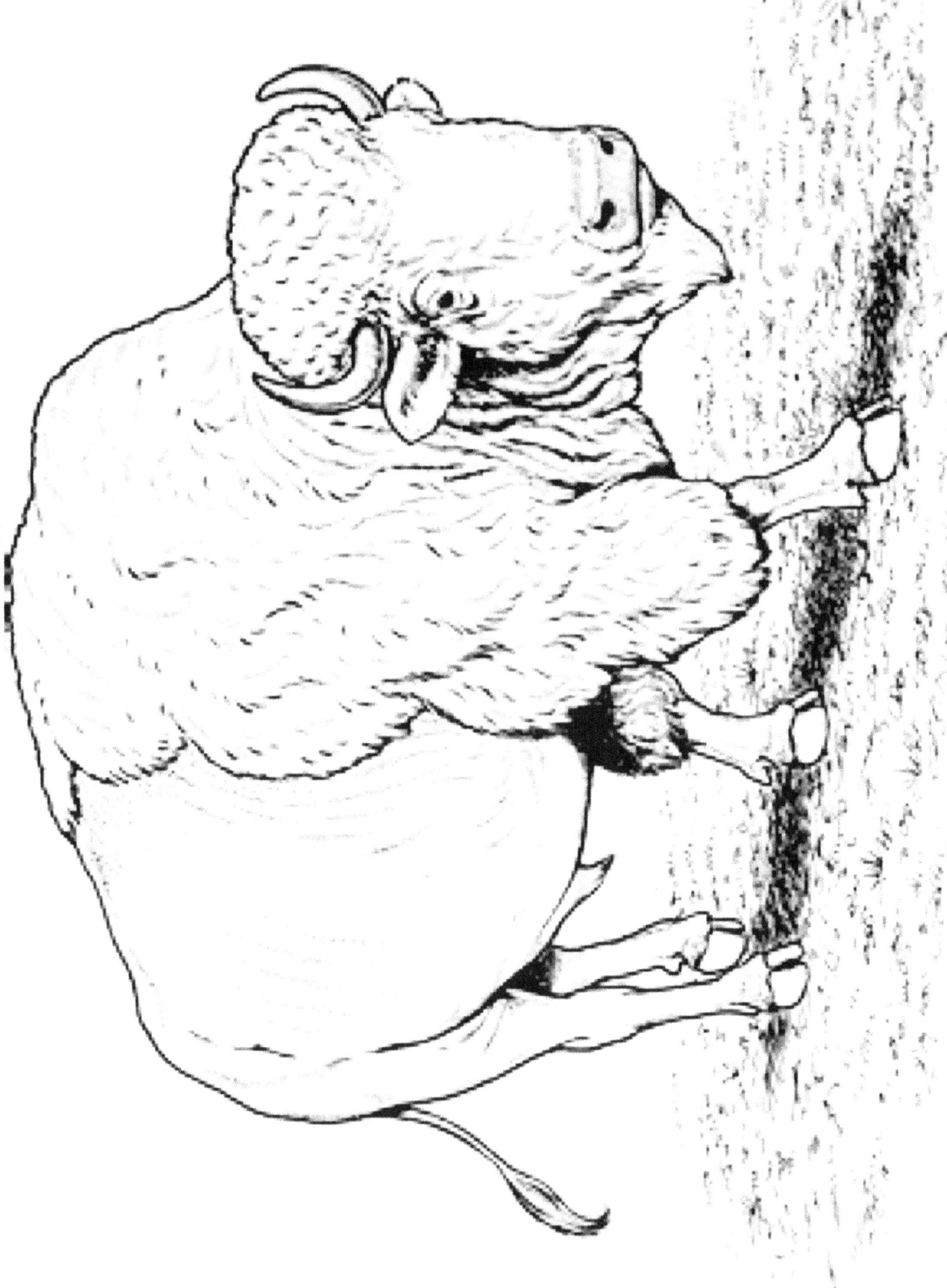